.

Power, Politics, and Print

Power, Politics, and Print

The Publication of the British
Museum Catalogue
1881-1900

Barbara McCrimmon

1981

LINNET BOOKS
HAMDEN, CONN

CLIVE BINGLEY
LONDON

© Barbara McCrimmon 1981

Published 1981 in the United States
as a Linnet Book,
an imprint of The Shoe String Press, Inc.,
Hamden, Connecticut 06514
and in the United Kingdom
by Clive Bingley Ltd.
16 Pembridge Road
London W11 3HL

LINNET ISBN 0-208-01874-3
BINGLEY ISBN 0 85157 3428

Library of Congress Cataloging in Publication Data

McCrimmon, Barbara.
    Power, politics, and print.
    Revision of the author's thesis, Florida State
University.
    Includes bibliographical references and index.
    1. British Museum. Dept. of Printed Books.
Catalogue of printed books in the library of the British
Museum. 2. British Museum. Dept. of Printed Books--
History--19th century. I. Title.
Z792.B863M33 1981   019'.1'0942142   80-28124
Linnet ISBN 0-208-01874-3
Bingley ISBN 0 85157 3428

Table of Contents

Preface

In the year 1879 a number of social, political, and internal forces came together at the British Museum in such a way as to result in the publication of the famous manuscript catalogue of the books in the general collections, compiled according to the "91 Rules." It was the first national library catalogue to be printed and so to become available in other libraries, and its importance in the bibliographic world has been enormous. To discover why and how such a historic event came about was the purpose of this study, which was undertaken as a dissertation for the Ph.D. degree at the Florida State University and which has been revised and shortened for publication.

The tale that unfolded from the research is one of frustration and contention, of small steady victories over inertia, and of a final triumph that came too late for celebration. The far-reaching results of the publication of the catalogue were never known by the men most responsible for the project. It is their story that needs to be told in its entirety, so far as it can be reconstructed from the documents they left behind and from relevant printed materials.

The documents are for the most part to be found in the archives of the British Museum library departments and those of the office of the principal librarian, later called the Director's Office. The term *library* was used to refer to both the Department of Printed Books and the Department of Manuscripts, but it was more generally confined to the Department of Printed Books, which included the Oriental books and manuscripts and the music collections.

The principal librarian was at the head of the entire institution. Over him was the board of trustees, which consisted of about fifty distinguished men. The archbishop of Canterbury, the lord chancellor, and the Speaker of the House of Commons were the "Principal Trustees" and had the most power. The rest were mostly peers of the realm, members of Parliament, leaders in the royal societies, and representatives of the families of the founders. The trustees delegated to a standing committee the general oversight of the Museum affairs. This committee delegated to a subcommittee on printed books and manuscripts, or "library subcommittee," the detailed deliberations necessary for bibliographic decisions, and to a subcommittee on finance, the burden of budgeting problems.

The heads of departments were called "keepers," and under them were two or three assistant keepers, several assistants, and attendants. The assistants were divided into upper and lower sections, initially in this study having a senior and a junior part to each section, making four classes in all, with differing rates of pay and prospects for advancement. These were later combined into two classes. There were also two sections of attendants, the higher one having clerical duties requiring good intelligence and capability, such as alphabetizing catalogue slips, the lower having less demanding tasks, such as fetching books for readers.

The records of the library departments have been preserved in "letter books," containing messages, announcements, records, and draft reports for the trustees. On the title page of the Department of Printed Books' letter book for 1875 is an announcement by Richard Garnett, dated 1893, that "the official documents from [1875] to 1888 inclusive were bound in 1889 on the plan adopted in the MS. Department, and have since been bound annually on the same system." The Department of Manuscripts' letter books were meticulously kept and set a high standard for the rest of the Museum. They were divided into sections by type of document, laid down in blank books, bound and folioed. The records of the Department of Printed Books, labeled "Minutes, Reports, Letters, etc.," are bound in one, two, or three volumes per year, those up to 1874 arranged chronologically, those after 1874 by type of document. [For a list of these sections, see p. 165.]

There was no foliation of the letter books of the Department of Printed Books until 1875, and from then on it was inconsistent. Some volumes were foliated in part, some not at all; some have two sets of numbers. It seemed best, therefore, in citing them, to ignore leaf numbers and refer simply to the date, author, and recipient of the message. The arrangement of the bound volumes is almost perfectly chronological, and where no date is given on the piece itself, the person who was responsible for arranging the pages for binding must be accepted as an authority on its placement.

The letter books of the Director's Office contain correspondence of the principal librarian and the trustees. Since the entire board met only once or twice a year, the minutes of the trustees' meetings consist chiefly of those of the standing committee and of the subcommittees. Their meetings were referred to as "committees" ("at a committee on April 12 . . .") and were numbered in sequence, with a "C," preceding ("C. 10, 191.") They are herein referred to as pages in the bound volumes: "p. 10, 191." The minutes themselves are available on microfilm as well.

The famed tradition of the accessibility of the British Museum's collections is fully carried out in the accessibility of its archives. The scholar must ever be appreciative of the care with which the records have been maintained and for the graciousness with which they are made available for research.

Permission to study and to quote from the archival material was given by the secretary of the Museum, on behalf of the trustees, and by the Department of Printed Books and the Department of Manuscripts. Research was completed shortly before these departments were separated administratively from the British Museum and became part of the British Library, Reference Division. At that time the archives were transferred to the British Library Board, and their assent to publication has also been secured.

For help in tracing the Bradshaw connection at the Cambridge University Library, I am indebted to Senior Under-Librarian for Special Collections, A. E. B. Owen. At the British Library, the letter books were, with considerable inconvenience, but unfailing good humor, procured from and returned to the vaults in the depths of the vast building by then Museum archivist Ann Hopley; by Olive N. Oldfield and her helpers in the Director's Office; by Pamela J. Willetts, deputy keeper in the Department of Manuscripts; and by the staff of the North Library, in cooperation with the personnel of the Ante-Room of the Keeper of Printed Books. R. J. Roberts, then assistant keeper in the department, now keeper of printed books in the Bodleian Library, Oxford, was also very obliging.

Most of all, it was Edward Miller, then an assistant keeper in the Department of Printed Books, later honorary archivist of the department, whose cooperation was essential to this study. Mr. Miller's writings on the British Museum provided a great fund of information, while his

Preface

willing and kindly personal advice extended through the present revision to a reading of the manuscript. For his sincere and generous interest in this book I will always be indebted, and I deeply regret that his untimely death prevented his seeing it in print.

Note

Full names, titles, and dates, when available, of persons mentioned in the text will be found in the index.

Introduction

During much of the nineteenth century the British literary public clamored for a printed catalogue of the British Museum library, but the century was over before the wish was fulfilled, and even when it was, the resulting work was not at all what had generally been expected. The person most responsible for the delay in committing the manuscript catalogue to print was Antonio Panizzi, who as keeper of printed books and then principal librarian was responsible for all matters connected with service to patrons of the reading room. Panizzi's goal was to get a definitive catalogue in manuscript, but his vigorous acquisitions policy made this a task of such giant proportions that it threatened to lock the library forever into a pattern of manual labor, ignoring the industrial revolution that had produced the books themselves and was about to make handwriting, if not obsolete, at least inefficient for the day-to-day business of scholarship.

John Winter Jones, who followed Panizzi in both offices, adhered strictly to his predecessor's pronouncements on cataloguing. In private he admitted that the bulk of the main catalogue was getting out of hand and that print was the only remedy, but he found himself unable to initiate a change. Instead, he left the solution of the matter to his successor, Edward Bond, who came from the Department of Manuscripts and had no commitments to anyone. Bond's tenure as principal librarian ended the Panizzian era, for although he had had excellent relations with Panizzi, Bond was intent on modernizing the British Museum. For a few months after taking office he deferred to the grand old leader, who was lying inert in his bed a few blocks away; but as soon as Panizzi died, Bond was ready to set in motion a plan for putting into print the titles of the new accessions in the Department of Printed Books. This was the thin edge of the wedge that opened the door to the printing, and then the publication, of the entire catalogue between 1880 and 1900. Bond was aided and abetted by Richard Garnett, assistant keeper and superintendent of the reading room, to whom the catalogue was a matter of deep concern from day to day and who had been waiting for the right moment to speak out.

There was one large stumbling block to the plans of Bond and Garnett: George Bullen, keeper of printed books, who, as a disciple of Panizzi, was not in sympathy with the printing project and whose resistance made the task of getting a printed catalogue more difficult. Bullen insisted on the completion in manuscript of Panizzi's great catalogue before the printing of it was begun. He preferred publishing individual headings such as "Shakespeare" and "Bible" to printing the entire catalogue; and, most of all, he favored the production of a catalogue of British printing up to the year 1640. He managed to promote this publication at a time when it interfered with the expedition of the larger work.

One reason for Bullen's concern with the catalogue of early English books was the advocacy of such a compilation by the Library Association of the United Kingdom, which, from its inception in 1877, had tried to promote national bibliographies of all the Western nations. With the support of organizations like the Royal Society for the Encouragement of Arts, Manufactures and Commerce, Britain's library leaders pressed the British Museum's officers either to produce the entire work, or else to supply the basic data for volunteers to complete. Meanwhile the Museum library was hard pressed to keep up with its normal routines, and could undertake no new projects without extra financial support from a traditionally conservative treasury.

Bond's persuasive powers were tested when he had to convince the trustees to petition the treasury for funds to begin the printing of the catalogue. Fortunately, it happened that out of the agitation for civil service reform, which had been going on for several decades, had come a suggestion by the treasury itself that money should be saved in government offices by substituting machines for men in making copies of communications and reports. Bond saw that printing the catalogue entries could be argued as an implementation of this idea. He thus found justification for the beginning of printing, and then assured support for the project through several political administrations by playing on their common concern for economy in government.

We must give the statesmen who were in power during the last two decades of the century their due for financing the printing of the British Museum catalogue; but beyond that the whole credit for the project must go to Bond and Garnett. They worked as a team, each contributing to the joint effort what he knew and could do best. It is doubtful whether either could have achieved the same results without the other, but it seems certain that the history of the British Museum would have been quite different without them both. They might be considered agents of a force that could not be stopped because its time had come, for the printing of library catalogues was going on apace and the pressure on the British Museum librarians to print theirs was intense. Yet it was Bond and Garnett who met the obstacles and conquered them with courage and intelligence, and the result was a remarkable accomplishment.

The end product of their effort was to be commonly referred to within the library as "GK 1," a term derived either from the German *Gesamt Katalog* ("entire or aggregate catalogue") or from "general" plus the Greek *Katalogos*. At the beginning of the revision of the old general catalogue according to the "91 Rules," Panizzi directed "that the letter K [for *Katalogos*] should be put in pencil to the heading. . . under which [the book] was catalogued"[1] in order to insure that no book would be left out of the new work. The need for such a device had been occasioned by the trustees' insistence on the production of the new catalogue letter-by-letter, rather than shelf-by-shelf, so that there was no assurance that every book in the library would be entered in it. By collating the newly written slips with the entries in the public catalogue, and marking those entries for which there were slips, a record could be kept of the completeness of the new general catalogue: the entries marked K were known to be in it. So began the use of the symbol K to refer to the work whose transformation into print is the subject of this study. Exactly when the evolving printed catalogue was dubbed "GK," or "GK 1," is not known, but is was many years ago .

Panizzi's insistence on accuracy above all, praiseworthy though it was in a day of lax bibiliographic standards, made the compiling of the manuscript catalogue a never-ending chore. It took the steady labor of many scholarly men over nearly fifty years to culminate in the copy from which "GK 1" was printed.

If the final published version of the catalogue was an unwieldy accretion of millions of entries that baffled those who had anticipated a few handy volumes, Panizzi could have told them it would be so. If its scope was frozen in time and space, so was that of many another reference work, and the British Museum catalogue was as useful as the best of them. If, despite precautions, it contained errors, Richard Garnett would have said this was inevitable, and less important than the fact that it existed at all.

Oddly enough, in 1847, when the trustees were agitating for a resumption of printing before the manuscript catalogue was complete, Panizzi had given his opinion that "it would take no less than thirty-five years to get the catalogue printed and, as it could not be ready before 1860, this meant 1895, a date by which most of those present would long have ceased to take any interest in the matter."[2] It is astonishing how close he came to predicting the actual date of completion of the printed catalogue, as well as the fact that those of its chief proponents still alive by then would be relatively indifferent to it.

I. The Panizzian Background

When the British Museum was young, its trustees planned to publish a catalogue of the printed books every twenty-five years. The handwritten catalogues of the Sloane and Royal libraries which existed when the Museum was incorporated in 1753 were supplemented in 1787 by a two-volume printed general catalogue drawn up by Samuel Ayscough, with the help of Paul Henry Maty and Samuel Harper. It is familiarly referred to as "Ayscough." This catalogue was afterward kept up-to-date by means of manuscript additions, and the whole was reedited by Henry Ellis and Henry Hervey Baber and published from 1813 to 1819 in seven volumes. The pages of two copies of this catalogue were mounted and bound into twenty-three-volume sets, with blank leaves interspersed for manuscript additions. One set was kept in the reading room and one in the staff workroom.

In 1834 it was deemed time to reprint the catalogue in order to include, not only the normal accessions, but also the contents of the large library of King George III, acquired ten years before. The Reverend Thomas Hartwell Horne had been working since 1831 on a classed catalogue

19

of the books, but it would take years to complete and was therefore to be abandoned in favor of a new alphabetical catalogue. To Baber, now the keeper of printed books, the ideal person to edit such a catalogue was Antonio Panizzi, who since entering the department in 1831 had proved the most energetic and skilful of the cataloguers. Indeed, Panizzi, who was set against classed catalogues, may have influenced the decision to revise the alphabetical catalogue and may have hoped to be its editor in chief. But the trustees rejected his candidacy and the work was begun by four assistants, of whom Panizzi was one. They proceeded assiduously for a year, and then stopped when an investigation into the condition of the Museum was undertaken by a select committee of the House of Commons. The committee reported in 1839 that "it is expedient that . . . full and accurate catalogues of all the collections in the Museum" should be made "with a view to print and publish such portions of them as would hold out expectations of even a partial sale."[1] The idea of publishing separate parts of the catalogue, such as author bibliographies, was favored by Panizzi and by many others, both within and without the Museum.

However, when Panizzi became keeper of printed books, on Baber's retirement in 1837, the trustees decided that the entire catalogue must be quickly printed, and Panizzi, with many misgivings, set his staff to work toward that goal. In 1841 the first volume, containing the letter *a*, appeared in print. The faults occasioned by its hasty compilation were so manifest that an embarrassed Panizzi ended the printing on his own initiative. Others might be willing to produce a "bad catalogue," but not he. First there must be an accurate catalogue of the entire library in manuscript, no matter how long it took to finish it. Panizzi was adamant on the point, and he thus set the framework within which the Department of Printed Books was to operate for the next forty years: a major proportion of departmental effort went continually into cataloguing and recataloguing. In order to expedite the manuscript catalogue, a troupe of newly hired transcribers, later to be called junior assistants, was set to rewriting all the entries in the interleaved Ellis and Baber catalogue. These had been adjusted by the senior assistants to conform to the new rules, and the juniors copied them onto thin paper, using a stylus to make three carbon copies. These copies of entries were then cut apart in strips called "title-slips," or just "titles" alphabetized, and mounted in folio volumes, half of each page being left blank for future additions. One set of volumes was placed in the main reading room for the use of patrons and two were used by the staff. The fourth copies of the entries were pasted on thicker paper strips and stored in boxes in shelf order.

By 1847 this manuscript catalogue was still only at the letter *d*, and the readers were making so many complaints that questions were asked in Parliament, and Panizzi became anxious to state his case in public. Criticisms were also made of the trustees' concentration on literature at the expense of science, and at last a royal commission was appointed to investigate the administration of the entire British Museum. Among the members of the commission were several Whigs who were friendly to Panizzi, but the Radical Joseph Hume wearied of the contention about the catalogue and threatened to call for a "return" to the House of Commons giving the author, title, and date of every book in the Museum library, which would make the catalogue into a parliamentary paper and guarantee its publication.

During the hearings of the commission, Panizzi put forth his views on the catalogue so convincingly that opposition to his method of compiling it collapsed. His primary object was to produce an alphabetical author catalogue meticulously and fully recorded from the books themselves for use within the library, and to finish it in

21

manuscript before undertaking to print any part of it. His loyal assistants in the Department of Printed Books who followed him in the keepership, and a majority of the trustees as well, were so persuaded of his wisdom that to go against his wishes came to seem heretical. Long after his retirement to a house in Bloomsbury Square, Panizzi's shadow fell over the department, and it did not begin to fade until his death. Even then, his power lingered in sufficient force to hamper publication of the catalogue once it was begun.

In 1866 Panizzi's faithful follower, John Winter Jones, took over as principal librarian, carrying on the Panizzian tradition and often seeking the master's advice on Museum problems. Jones had been born into a family of editors and authors and had been trained for the law, which gave him a bond with Panizzi. Forced by illness to abandon a legal career, he studied languages and literature and came to the British Museum in April 1837, two months before Panizzi was made keeper of printed books. He became an eager assistant in all the changes that were wrought in the Museum in the ensuing years and was particularly adept at cataloguing, taking a prominent part in the deliberations that resulted in the "91 Rules," and being designated "general reviser" of the entries for the new catalogue according to those rules. As he followed Panizzi up the administrative ladder, to keeper in 1856 and to principal librarian ten years later, he lost effectiveness, and in the latter position he directed the Museum in a quiet phase of consolidation after the turbulence of Panizzi's incumbency.

Unfortunately, the quiet turned out to be deceptive, for beneath the surface anger and frustration seethed among the lower staff over their wages, duties, and working environment. They were plodding along with the catalogue, but as if on a treadmill, never seeming to get ahead. Jones had been followed in the keepership, at one remove, by William Brenchley Rye, who had been a fellow law student with Jones and had been recommended by him for a job as transcriber at the Museum in 1838. Rye had become a protégé of Panizzi and had performed various duties in the department, especially the arranging of collections and the selecting and cataloguing of the reference books in the reading room. He was more of an antiquarian than some of his colleagues, having edited several historical works, and in administration he was a traditionalist, following Panizzi's precedents. In the seventies he began to lose his sight and to develop other ailments, and he let the affairs of the department slip until there occurred a minor revolt among the junior assistants.

Staff Ferment

The grand building designed by Sir Robert Smirke for the British Museum had been conceived by him as a monument, and it contained scanty accommodation for the staff. As the Museum's collections and the number of employees grew, therefore, the effects of the building's flaws were intensified. Transcribers sat shivering under three drafty windows recently installed in the stone-floored basement room allotted to them; yet, they said, without the windows the place would be stuffy. Cataloguers hunched on high stools in corners of the stacks under a remote skylight that failed them utterly on foggy days. If the former got sick and the latter had to be dismissed for the day because of the lack of light, the progress of the library's work suffered.

At last, on April 13, 1874, several of the men asked for a raise in salary and at the same time petitioned for some remedy to the ventilation of the basement room, known to them as the "tank" or "den," in which twenty transcribers wrote their slips. They claimed to have been made ill by the faulty windows. Keeper Rye replied that the reasons for absence given by these men since 1868 had had no connection with ventilation: one of them had been out for five months as a result of a fall suffered when chasing a fire engine; another had sprained an ankle in a "high jump."[2] This argument prevailed with the trustees, for although in June some raises were granted by the treasury, nothing was done to better the working environment of the transcribers.

A year later, however, when the junior assistants again protested the "unhealthy sanitary conditions" and the "cold, gloomy"[3] rooms where they had to work, Rye supported their petition. The trustees responded by sending a delegation to visit the museum and survey the facilities, after which it was recommended that the men be allowed to work in one of the reading rooms in the North Wing. During the spring, the inspector for air pollution from the Local Government Board made "a great number of experiments in the ventilation of the Museum"[4] and projected further tests during the coming winter.

But in March 1875, the situation came to a head over a trifling event. A pamphlet entitled "The Actual Condition of the British Museum; a Literary Expostulation" was published, to be hawked on the streets for a shilling, by Stefan Poles, a scapegrace refugee, who was annoyed by the Museum's acquisition of a pamphlet denouncing him. He had been briefed by one of the disgruntled assistants on their complaints, and there he concentrated his attack . The result was described by Rye as " a right good slather against the B M and its administrators."[5] Poles charged Jones and the library officers with favoritism, poor management, and waste of public funds. "The library is managed by a clique of jobbing ignoramuses,"[6] he said, whose "work consists in the exchanging of reports on reports and letters on letters."[7] He denounced the unhealthy, unsightly, and uncomfortable surroundings in which the junior members of the staff were forced to spend their days, and gave his version of the catalogue problem: twenty-five men were devoting their whole time to cataloguing, yet it progressed at a snail's pace; Rye was supposed to inspect their work, but was always too busy; up to that time the catalogue had cost £200,000, the cost simply of pasting new slips into the volumes being £2,500 a year.

These criticisms may have been exaggerated and malicious, but their impact could not be ignored. Rye was recovering from an eye operation and in April was "quite prostrate with pleurisy or rheumatism or something like it in my left leg,"[8] so he had grounds for retiring on account of health, which he did on June 14. His long time colleague, George Bullen, became keeper of printed books.

George Bullen

Bullen had been born in Ireland, though he had lived in England most of his life, and, unlike some of his colleagues, was easygoing and had a pleasant temperament. After starting out as a school teacher, he had come to the British Museum in 1838 and had been assigned to help arrange the books on the shelves of the new library building just completed by Smirke. He subsequently worked on the catalogue, compiling the large heading "Aristotle" for the 1841 printed volume. In 1850 he was promoted to senior assistant and in 1866 to the joint office of assistant keeper and superintendent of the reading room, where he made many friends among the readers, being praised for his affable manner as well as for his knowledge of the books in the library. It was a natural step upward from there to the keepership.

As an expert on early printing, Bullen was given responsibility for the catalogue of the Caxton loan exhibition in South Kensington in 1877, and that of the Martin Luther exhibit which he arranged in the Grenville collection at the British Museum in 1883. He also compiled catalogues of two outside libraries. In 1892 he edited a facsimile of a unique Caxton which had been acquired under his keepership, and during his professional life he contributed many articles to the influential *Athenaeum* magazine.

Bullen was one of the founders of the Library Association, having been a member of the organizing council, and later served as a vice-president. He was a fellow of the Society of Antiquaries and received an honorary LL.D. from Glasgow University upon his retirement. He was created C.B. in 1899. His name was suggested for the principal librarianship in 1878 and again in 1888, but on both occasions the trustees preferred to recommend to the queen a man from the Department of Manuscripts.

According to all evidence, Bullen was well liked by his subordinates. One of them wrote to him, on a question of cataloguing, "I have not offered any apology for troubling you, not because I think that none is due, but because you never allow us to feel that a claim on your help or sympathy or direction in such matters requires one."[9] This indicates that channels of communication in the department had been opened when Bullen became keeper. When he retired, the attendants as well as the assistants presented him with testimonials and a silver tea service.

Nevertheless, more ambitious men, such as Richard Garnett, found Bullen's relaxed attitude toward administration and his adherence to Panizzi's cataloguing principles frustrating. Bullen reigned as keeper for fifteen years, and during that time stirring events occurred in the Museum and in the library world. He was swept into them, yet he retained a traditional outlook in the face of the changes going on around him; and it was entirely without enthusiasm that he presided over the publication of the general catalogue of the printed books between 1879 and his retirement in 1890.

He was compelled to support this project against his better judgment when John Winter Jones turned over the direction of the British Museum to men who had a more modern concept of the role of the institution in the nation and the world. In 1877 Jones's health began to fail and he sought the milder air of Cornwall for the winter months, leaving Charles Thomas Newton of the Department of Greek and Roman Antiquities in charge. Although he was a favorite of Panizzi, Newton was more forward-looking than Jones, and during his few months as acting principal librarian he brought the question of printing the general catalogue to the attention of the trustees. But Jones returned in April of 1878 and remained through August, and only after that could any lasting progress be made.

II. The Leadership of Edward Bond

There was nothing about Edward Augustus Bond to signal the hero, for he was a quiet, modest, and ingratiating scholar with little discernable ambition. Nevertheless, he was to play the heroic role in getting the British Museum catalogue into print, for, when he found himself in power, he became a dynamic promoter of change.

Bond's father had been master of a large school for boys and, at the same time, chaplain to the duke of Kent, Queen Victoria's father, for whom Edward was named. After attending the Merchant Taylors' School, Bond at seventeen became an assistant in the Public Record Office, which was then in the Tower of London and which was in a state of confusion from lack of strong administration. It provided an object lesson in poor management which was not lost on the intelligent young man. All the same, Bond there received his foundation training in early handwriting from the able Sir Thomas Duffus Hardy.

At the age of twenty-three, Bond moved to the Department of Manuscripts at the British Museum to work under one of the greatest of paleographers, Sir Frederic Madden. He was soon set to the task of "seeing through the press the general index to the manuscript catalogues in the Reading Room,"[1] a major effort which demonstrated most of the problems of cataloguing. Madden found him a "most efficient and most praiseworthy assistant."[2] In 1852 Bond was honored by being given the title and the extra salary of "Egerton Librarian," derived from the trust established for the collection of manuscripts donated by the Reverend Francis Egerton, eighth earl of Bridgewater. In 1854 he succeeded to the position of assistant keeper of the department, and for the next twelve years he not only carried an administrative load, but also acted as a messenger and go-between for the feuding keeper of manuscripts, Madden, and the principal librarian, Panizzi. That both parties to the quarrel respected and liked Bond is testimony to his diplomacy, which proved to be an even greater asset in later years.

Bond also found time for editorial work. At government request he edited the *Speeches in the Trial of Warren Hastings*, published in four volumes from 1859 to 1861, an arduous task which "permanently affected his health and spirits."[3] He had previously edited for the Hakluyt Society two works on travel in Russia in the sixteenth century (1856), and for the Rolls Series he edited the *Chronicle of Meaux Abbey* (1868).

When Madden retired, at the same time as Panizzi, in 1866, Bond became keeper of manuscripts, in the usual order of succession. Once given authority, he established a "high standard of regularity and efficiency"[4] in the department. He proceeded quickly to attack the arrears of cataloguing, which had been allowed to lag while Madden concentrated on sorting fragments of Cottonian manuscripts burned in the fire of 1731. In June of 1867 Bond gave a report to the trustees on the state of the department and elicited their approval for his plans: he discontinued the printing of accessions lists, customary since 1831, and undertook instead an index to the lists already in print;

then he ordered that the entries of the several printed catalogues of individual manuscript collections be arranged into a combined classed catalogue, which has been of great value to scholars throughout the years, although it has never been printed.

To prosecute the new work, Bond asked for an extra assistant, but the trustees did not accede to his request. Then he initiated the practice of employing assistants after official hours to catalogue and index, as it was considered to be less expensive to pay for overtime than to add another full salary to the budget. Extra funds were granted to pay for the indexing in this way of the acquisitions since 1848, of the catalogues of the Sloane and Birch collections, and of the charters and rolls. Bond introduced into his department the "Wedgwood carbonic manifold writer" for transcription of catalogue titles, in order to get four copies for each writing, as was done in the Department of Printed Books. When the classed catalogue was completed in 1874, the printing of accessions lists was resumed.

Bond thus left his greatest mark in the area of cataloguing, but he showed perspicacity in other ways as well, as in securing promotion for Edward Maunde Thompson, who had entered the department in 1861 and who was to follow Bond as keeper and then as principal librarian. Together they worked to establish the unsettled date of the Utrecht Psalter, and then, in 1873, founded the Palaeographical Society for similar studies. As a project of the society, they shared the editing of four volumes of *Facsimiles of Ancient Charters in the British Museum* and three of *Facsimiles of Manuscripts and Inscriptions* from 1873 to 1878. These were photographic reproductions, one of the earliest uses of the camera in scholarly work, and provide evidence of Bond's continuing interest in mechanical aids to scholarship. He even had the boldness, in 1872, to request that the trustees apply to the government for an annual grant to purchase the enormous library of the late

made less stringent under Bond. The two "closed days" when only art and science students had been admitted for study were restricted to the particular galleries they frequented; the ban on children in arms was rescinded; and the necessity of renewing reading tickets every six months was withdrawn. Bond also suggested that the trustees allow the Museum's exhibits to be used for teaching small classes of elementary students.

Such democracy was not to Winter Jones's taste, as he remarked to an admirer of Panizzi in a letter from his retirement home near Exeter: "I am sorry to read what you say about the Museum. I fear that there is too great a desire to court popularity and that the high objects for which the institution was founded may be lost sight of."[16] On the contrary, Bond was carrying out the directions of the original act of incorporation of the British Museum: "That a free access ... to the Collections ... shall be given to all studious and curious persons."[17] The studious had always been favored over the curious in the implementation of the admission policy, but Bond was responding to the general extension downwards of traditional class privileges, and there were many who appreciated his efforts, such as the editor of the *Athenaeum*, who wrote, "Mr. Bond is fulfilling the hopes of those who believed that his accession to the chief post of the Museum would be the signal for important reforms."[18]

On one occasion, however, Bond's desire to increase the accessibility of the institution caused a small crisis in the Department of Printed Books. It had been customary to close the Museum for three weeks each year for general cleaning; but in 1881, Bond told the heads of departments that he planned to reduce the closed time to two weeks. Bullen replied that his department had always fully used the period for verifying the registers of all returned books and slips and for reading the shelves, and that if the time were reduced, verification would have to be continuous, which would require an extra attendant. Another duster would be needed, also, with an attendant paid to supervise him, if all the books were to be dusted in two weeks. These arguments failed to change Bond's mind or to produce more workers. Instead, Garnett, acting for Bullen, had hastily to circularize the other departments in order to call in the thousand-odd books from the library that were being used elsewhere in the building. He asked that they be returned "tomorrow, September 28."[19] The departments complied, and this massive transfer was made successfully on one day's notice.

Bond was constantly concerned about the working conditions, salaries, and fringe benefits of the staff, even down to the dusters, in response to a memorial, or petition, from whom he wrote out a four-page letter. His diligence in investigating such requests extended to consulting past minutes of the standing committee of the trustees, for on the Department of Printed Books' copy of a minute of June 14, 1884, allowing the customary extra two weeks' holiday to the assistant R. E. Graves on the occasion of his marriage, is a laconic note added in Bond's hand in red ink: "Mem. Mr. Graves was allowed a fortnight's vacation on his marriage in 1862. C. 10, 191."[20]

In such ways Bond involved himself in the details of Museum business to a greater extent than might have been expected of a principal librarian, and he concentrated much of his attention on the Department of Printed Books. He called two meetings in the spring of 1879 with the keeper and assistant keepers to discuss ways to improve the reading room service. At one of these meetings, he got the keepers to agree to consider discontinuing some periodicals and some publications of academies. At the other, he requested that assistants be encouraged to point out desiderata in their areas of specialization "without stopping the duties of Cataloguing."[21] He recommended the hiring of boys to carry books for the reading room—"trotters," they were called—and he personally selected them. After setting their minimum age at fifteen years in the beginning, he secured permission from the trustees, the treasury, and the civil service commissioners to increase the minimum age to sixteen, with the same qualifying examination requirement as for the men attendants, though at the previous low rate of pay, twelve shillings a week.[22]

On other occasions Bond suggested that Bullen request for the library a copy of the minutes of the senate of the University of London since 1856,[23] and pointed out a number of books with Department of Printed Books press marks "which he considered unsuitable for the Map Department."[24] He also criticized the revision of the "91 Rules," which was begun in 1884, as being too elaborate: he had in mind the publication of the rules for use by readers, whereas the departmental purpose was to make them more precise for the convenience of the cataloguers.[25] A similar incident involved G. K. Fortescue and the first of his alphabetical subject lists of accessions. These were easier to compile and to search than a classed catalogue, which was more complex and needed a key. But Bond had made

> a really very useful Classed Catalogue of all the Manuscripts, and was prejudiced in favor of this form. Thus it was that, though he took every interest in Fortescue's work, his well-meant interference, always in favour of large subject headings, gave a good deal of trouble in the making of the first quinquennial volume, which was certainly not so good as its successors. . . .[26]

The term "well-meant interference" is particularly appropriate to describe the combination of enthusiasm for progress with oversedulous concern in departmental affairs that marked Bond's administrative style. His constant interest in the management of the Department of

Printed Books undoubtedly kept Bullen under a certain amount of strain.

During Bond's principal librarianship, nevertheless, great advances were made at the British Museum. The achievement of print for the general catalogue of books will be treated in detail in subsequent chapters. He was also responsible for a most welcome addition to the main building, the White Wing, built between 1880 and 1885 partly with funds bequeathed to the Museum sixty years before by a Mr. William White. Since the construction consisted of enclosing part of the principal librarian's garden, it must have entailed a considerable sacrifice of convenience for the Bond family in the interest of a better British Museum. Such improvements were carried forward by Bond with a characteristic "driving force."[27]

Richard Garnett

Bond's ally in the printing of the catalogue, Richard Garnett, is remembered as one of the most likable men in the Museum during his forty-eight years there. His father, a clergyman and philologist, had been an assistant keeper in the Department of Printed Books from 1838 until his death in 1851. To help ease the family's financial plight after his loss, Panizzi then secured an appointment in the department for the sixteen-year-old son. The youth began by copying titles for the new catalogue and soon was made a cataloguer, for he had followed his father's example by becoming an accomplished linguist through self-instruction.

When Rye became assistant keeper in 1857, Garnett was chosen to be his helper in classifying and arranging the books as they came in. Rye gradually became involved in other duties and left the "placing" more and more to Garnett, who at last did the work alone. His conduct in this very responsible position earned for him the respect of both Panizzi and Rye. The latter wrote of him:

I ought to say that for the efficient discharge of this duty, which involved the accurate classification of perhaps 3000 or 4000 books annually in all languages and on all subjects there is required a considerable linguistic knowledge, a wide range of general information, as well as an acquaintance with literary history. . . . I may add that I have frequently derived very valuable assistance from him in replying to questions on points of scholarship and literary history which have been officially addressed to me during my term of Keepership. It may not be superfluous to say that in point of temper, tact, and courtesy, Mr. Garnett possesses qualifications which are very desirable in an officer of a large public establishment.[28]

The task of placer was ideal for a quiet, book-loving person like Garnett. He thoroughly enjoyed looking into each volume to ascertain its proper location on the shelves according to its subject. Blessed with a retentive memory, he had no difficulty in recalling what he had learned in this way, even many years after the sight of the book. Such a faculty made him an outstanding candidate for the role of superintendent of the reading room, as Rye acknowledged in the recommendation quoted. However, his gaining the honor in 1875 meant exchanging the peaceful environment of the stacks for a place of strenuous activity, human bustle, and constant challenge. Garnett filled this office with distinction for nine years, putting to use his remarkable knowledge of books and literature in a way that became legendary. As an example of the "living catalogue" librarian he knew no equal, at least in a library of such immense size and scope. A visitor to the reading room at this time later recalled:

At the centre of it all, the head spider in this great web used to sit—Mr. Richard Garnett, who always impressed me as the most good-natured man in the world. However absurd the questions brought him by foolish people, or however difficult the inquiries made to him by the wise ones, he was always ready with a cordial smile to do the best he could, and to take any amount of trouble for anyone who asked. . . . I think the greatest man in England could have no more cordiality from this model official than he gave to the humblest.[29]

A colleague at the Museum gave a slightly different view, saying that Garnett knew "when to give special help to readers and when to snub them, and few could do either more effectively. . . ."[30] Another acquaintance said that Garnett showed "extra courtesy . . . to the forlorn-looking: to those not blessed with this world's goods or . . . success,"[31] indicating that his snubs may have been reserved for the haughty or arrogant. Yet he earned the praise of all classes of patrons, and in an unusual gesture, the "frequenters of the Reading Room,"[32] when he left them to edit the catalogue, presented him with a testimonial illuminated in the style of a medieval manuscript.

Garnett was so tall that he usually had to bend down to talk in his quiet tone to others, and younger members of the staff were sufficiently awed by his stature and his dignified demeanor to feel some constraint before him. "Gentle, easy of approach, and entirely unassuming as he was, it may be doubted whether any man ever ventured to take a liberty with him,"[33] said one of them; and a grandson recalled that "when he was in his sixties, he was assailed by three young ruffians in Endell Street and wielded [his umbrella] so vigorously that he put them to flight."[34] An acquaintance noted that Garnett's placid bearing could be suddenly and startlingly shattered. "That he might explode never crossed my mind. But at a meeting when a member let out a maladroit word or two he made us all jump by thundering out the word 'Bosh!'"[35] Equally unexpected could be a flash of droll, and often ironic, wit—his way of expressing his awareness of humanity's follies and foibles.

Although he was not a forceful speaker, Garnett used language with a rare felicity and was frequently called upon to speak for the British Museum library. He was active in the Library Association from the start and served as its president in 1892-93. He was also a founder and a president of the Bibliographical Society. Furthermore, he was a prolific writer, a minor poet, and a literary critic. He published, for example, nine books of verse; biographies of Carlyle, Emerson, Coleridge, Milton, and Blake; a *History of Italian Literature; English Literature, An Illustrated Record*, with Edmund Gosse; and editions of various literary works, as well as a book of short stories and two volumes of essays and speeches. He contributed widely to periodicals, to the *Dictionary of National Biography* and to the ninth edition of the *Encyclopaedia Britannica*. Most of his major prose works are still in print, some of them having been brought out by facsimile reprint houses in recent years. He also edited a series of library manuals. He suggested the adoption of the sliding press at the Museum after he had discovered it in another library, and he was always alert to possibilities for improving the efficiency of operation and the service to the public of the Department of Printed Books.

Garnett was a tireless worker who was proud that he had never missed a day of duty through illness. When he undertook to edit the volumes of the general catalogue for the press, he worked at all hours, in the Museum and at home. Yet despite his energetic labor and all his favorable qualities, he was twice passed over for promotion. The second time it was in favor of a man two years his junior in service, and Garnett was indignant and ready to resign. Then at the inception of the printing program which he had so prominently favored, the orientalist Robert Kennaway Douglas was chosen to superintend it. Douglas had compiled and seen through the press a catalogue of the

Chinese books in the library, and Bond had "great confidence"[36] in him. Nevertheless, one would expect the selection of the editor to have been based on seniority and commitment, where Garnett excelled. It may have been a reaction to these slights that led him to apply for the vacant Bodleian librarianship in 1882, though by then he was pretty much in charge of the catalogue publication project. Fortunately for the British Museum, he was not successful, and he remained in the Department of Printed Books for the rest of his working years. Some solace came to him in the form of an LL.D. from the University of Edinburgh in 1883, and the C. B. in 1895.

During all but the last nine years of Garnett's tenure George Bullen was his superior, yet it was Garnett who had the greater influence on the future of the institution, and who was, in Edward Miller's phrase, "to dominate, in his own way, the next generation at the Museum, as Panizzi had done his."[37] He was the most active proponent of the printed catalogue, and that was to be his chief monument in the library world. Of that catalogue a colleague commented:

> The credit . . . due to his friend and chief, the late Sir E. A Bond, has been so emphasized that future readers may hardly realize how essentially its initiation and execution have been Dr. Garnett's own work. From the moment it was mooted to the day on which he laid down office, it was his chief concern that nothing, however desirable in itself, should be allowed to stand in its way or hinder its rapid progress, and to this determination on his part its success is undoubtedly due.[38]

The History of the Catalogue

At the Cambridge meeting of the Library Association in September 1882, Garnett read an account of "The Printing

41

of the British Museum Catalogue,"[39] in which he traced the early history of the catalogue and then the more recent events leading to the situation at the time of the meeting. The essence of the latter part of the story may be summarized as follows.

When the revised catalogue compiled under Panizzi's direction was placed in the reading room in 1851 it consisted of 150 volumes. It contained the entries from the Ellis and Baber catalogue along with those for the books acquired since its publication, the two groups of entries having to be amalgamated continually. At that time the great flood of books to be brought in by Panizzi's large purchase grants and the enforcement of the copyright had barely begun, and printing all the titles would have been comparatively easy; but Panizzi was not interested.

Ten years later the adoption by the Cambridge University Library of print for accessions presented a challenge to the British Museum library to do the same. The challenge was not met, and by 1869 there were fifteen hundred volumes of the catalogue in the reading room. The new keeper, Rye, claimed to be strongly in favor of committing them to print; but the trustees decided to wait for the completion of the amalgamating process, although the influx of new books made that object recede farther every day.

The treasury, which had protested the cost of rebinding the catalogue volumes on more than one occasion, finally, in October of 1875, requested a report on the advantages and disadvantages of printing them. Garnett, in his new capacity as assistant keeper and superintendent of the reading room, was asked to make the report, and in it he pressed for print on the grounds of the fast-diminishing space in the reading room for shelving the catalogue. There were by then two thousand volumes plus the catalogues of maps and music, all ranged in concentric circles around the central staff desk area. Garnett proposed printing all the accession titles immediately, as the books came in, while planning a way to put the whole catalogue into type.

In January 1878, the treasury again raised the subject, and Garnett again, this time with the encouragement of Newton, sent the trustees a memorandum giving the reasons for what he considered by then to be the stark necessity to print. But the difference in point of view between the staff of the Museum and the trustees is reflected in the expedient adopted to avoid the inevitable decision a while longer: civil service writers were hired at a low rate of pay to try to hurry up the transcription of the old titles for amalgamation.

Then Bond took office as principal librarian, and the atmosphere changed. In April 1879, the *New Quarterly Magazine* carried an article by Garnett[40] which stated the arguments for putting the catalogue into type. That summer the trustees capitulated to print for accessions, the treasury agreed, and in January 1880, the entries began to come from the press.

Still, Garnett's main goal, to get the whole catalogue into printed form, was held back by Bullen's catalogue of early English books, which required large amounts of staff time, while the final revision of the manuscript general catalogue, "the indispensable preliminary to a completed printed catalogue, was so languidly prosecuted that it seemed in danger of coming to a standstill."[41] It took some energetic action on the part of Edward Bond, with Garnett's help, to get the stalled cataloguing work under way in a more efficient fashion.

These are the main outlines of the story. Before filling in the details, we must look at some other areas of endeavor that bore on the inauguration of the printing program.

III. The Political Background

The 1870s and 1880s were turbulent decades politically in Great Britain, full of cries for the reform of customs based on privilege, with minority groups struggling for recognition and with human rights beginning to appear as a popular cause. One of the most active political pressure groups was the lower civil service, including the staff of the British Museum, who had attained that desirable status under Panizzi and who were directly affected by the agitation among their fellows in other government agencies.

Although it was necessary, under either party, for the treasury to operate "within extremely narrow fiscal bounds,"[1] if the system of free trade, on which the economy was based, were to flourish, still the choices of programs to favor depended at least in part on the tastes and interests of the persons in whom the power of decision was vested. Therefore, the characters of the officers of the treasury were of importance in their confrontation with their subordinates.

Between 1868 and 1885 the government was alternately led by the two greatest political figures of the era, the arch-rivals William Ewart Gladstone and Benjamin Disraeli, each of whom had been chancellor of the exchequer as well as prime minister. Gladstone, who carried his intense religious devotion into his public life, felt that the overseer of the public purse was answerable to God for the uncompromisingly earnest protection of his charge. He was a master of finance who could hold listeners spellbound when he explained the budget, a manipulator of details, a demander of precision from subordinates, and an exemplar of the twelve-hour work day who left his rigorous mark on the office of the exchequer. Says one commentator, "Gladstone was filled with a passion for economy in public spending so fierce that at times he does not seem to be entirely sane on that subject. Certainly both he and the British Treasury, over which he so often presided, seem on occasion to have lost all sense of proportion."[2] The staff of the British Museum were to feel the thrust of this statement, albeit at a time when Gladstone was out of office.

The Conservative Disraeli did not share the Liberal Gladstone's extreme frugality in financial matters, but he left most of the budgeting to his subordinates, and he chose as his chancellor of the exchequer a Gladstone-trained man. As to reform, Disraeli was more interested in altering social than political affairs, yet he claimed to have been the first to use the term "administrative reform"[3] in reference to his party's attempts to increase the efficiency of government departments, a cause with which Gladstone later became identified. It was around this cause that the controversy over the civil service developed, both employer and employees wanting change, but for quite opposite reasons.

During the Gladstone and Disraeli ministries, not only was the civil service regulated more fairly, but modernization took place in education, public health and housing, pollution control, food and drug regulation, courts, and elections. Workers gained the right to organize and to strike, among other benefits. Yet finance was difficult throughout these years, and pressure for economy in government offices and institutions was taken up by both parties as a noncontroversial way to lower public spending. Unfortunately, controversy did develop, and the savings effected were insignificant for the amount of grief they caused.

Gladstone as Trustee

Both these prime ministers were trustees of the British Museum, and both were devoted to its prosperity. Therefore, it is not surprising that, despite all difficulties, their treasuries agreed to the proposal to print the Museum library catalogue. Little has been recorded about Gladstone's trusteeship, but he was as attentive to the affairs of the Museum as his heavy schedule would allow. When not in office he was a member of the standing committee, and he was on the subcommittee on finance from 1875 to 1876. Strict though he was about accountability, Gladstone was generous in his attitude toward acquisitions for the Museum and he was always in favor of a separate building for the scientific collections. In 1859, when Richard Owen, superintendent of natural history at the Museum, publicized his desire for such a solution to the overcrowding in his departments, he sent Gladstone, then chancellor of the exchequer, a copy of his statement on the matter. Possibly urged on by his friend, Principal Librarian Panizzi, Gladstone thereupon paid a visit to the Museum and went around the natural history sections, as well as the basement storage rooms, with Owen, exhibiting a characteristic thoroughness in his inspection, as Owen described it:

He explored with me every vault and dark recess which had been, or could be, allotted to the non-exhibited specimens of the natural history, those, viz., which it was my aim to utilize and bring to light. He gave the same attention to the series selected for exhibition in the public galleries, and appreciated the inadequacy of the arrangements to that end. He listened to my statements of facts, . . . tested every averment, and elicited the grounds of every suggestion, with a tact and insight that contrasted strongly with the questionings in the [trustees'] committee-room, where too often vague interrogations met with answers to match.[4]

Once convinced of the good sense of Owen's ideas, Gladstone moved quickly to implement them. A month after his tour of the Museum, he put the treasury on record as approving the expense of removing the natural history collections to a site of their own; and a month after that he packed a special general meeting of the trustees, who "found themselves confronted by the unexpected attendance of the ex-officio trustees who represented the government,"[5] and secured their confirmation of his motion for the separation of the two parts of the Museum—the sciences from the humanities. In spite of this efficient action, it was to be twenty long years before the new building could be occupied and the desired relief from the crowding of the collections in the old building could actually be felt.

Disraeli as Trustee

Disraeli had been unanimously elected to the board of trustees in September 1863, on the grounds of his "literary eminence" as well as his position in the House of Commons and, as Lord Palmerston delicately phrased it, "whereas many of the existing Trustees belong more or less to one political party, it was desirable that the choice to be made should show that party politics are not to be permitted to enter within the gates of a building dedicated to Learning and to the Arts."[6] In his note of acceptance, Disraeli remarked that his father, Isaac D'Israeli, was "the first man of letters who, much more than half a century ago, began to turn [the Museum's] MS. wealth to account in the illustration of our history, and I have been brought up in a due appreciation of its treasures and a due reverence for its authorities."[7] He might have added that he had been issued a reader's ticket at the age of sixteen. Disraeli's chief biographer says that he

> attended with assiduity to his duties as a Trustee, and when in office never forgot the interests of the Museum. It was mainly due to his clear-sightedness and promptitude that the wonderful Blacas Collection in Paris, which, with its wealth of gems and cameos, the French Emperor was anxious to keep for France, was secured for England and the British Museum at the cost of £48,000....Another matter in which he specially interested himself was the securing for the British Museum, during the 1874 Ministry, of the Castellani Collection, including the fine bronze head of Venus. In fact, his record as Trustee and as Minister is one for which the Museum has reason to be grateful.[8]

Disraeli also recorded, in a letter to Lady Bradford, his pride in the first of these purchases, which had been made when he was chancellor of the exchequer in the Derby government.

> I always remember with delight that in 1867-8, on my own responsibility, I bought for the nation the Blacas collection of gems—£50,000!
> If I could give our gallery some pictures of equal

quality, [I] would not have lived in vain.[9]

His memory was faulty, because it was in November 1866, while Parliament was in recess, that he had daringly contracted for the Blacas purchase. Fortunately, the money for it was granted by the House of Commons on February 18, 1867.[10] He also slightly exaggerated the price. Charles Newton, upon whose suggestion and through whose agency the purchase was made, had apparently been given leave by Disraeli to bid as high as £50,000 if necessary, but had needed to go only to £48,000. Then some items in the collection which were duplicates of Museum possessions were sold, so that the final sum voted was £45,721. Gladstone spoke in favor of confirming the chancellor's presumptuous action in committing such a large sum without permission; thus he helped to assure the appropriation, surely more for the good of the nation and the Museum than out of kindness toward his opponent.

In 1874 Disraeli did acquire some Italian Renaissance paintings for the National Gallery, as he told Lady Bradford, in the letter quoted, that he wanted to do; but he also drew the criticism of a member of the board of trustees of the British Museum, Lord Acton, who wrote to Panizzi that from the point of view of attempts to better the organization of the Museum, "Disraeli was quite useless on the Board."[11] This may have been because, as Disraeli himself recounted, he had left his country house in January 1874 to travel to London to attend a meeting of the trustees, only to learn that Prime Minister Gladstone had called for an election, and he quickly forgot the meeting in his determination to see that his party won.[12] His efforts were so successful that by February he was himself prime minister, and during his term of office the printing of the catalogue of the British Museum library was begun.

The Political Background

The Treasury

More immediately in control of the finances of the British Museum were the chancellors of the exchequer. Gladstone's chancellor in his first ministry, 1868-74, was Robert Lowe, who, as a trustee of the Museum, proved to be less solicitous of the interests of its staff than might have been expected. In 1855, after a career in Australia and then a seat in the House of Commons, Lowe had been made vice-president of the Board of Trade, the cradle of chancellors of the exchequer. In 1868 he was given the higher post by Gladstone, who had made the same transition, and they worked harmoniously together. Nevertheless, Lowe's harsh manner and love of blunt argument made him unpopular in many quarters, and when, in the summer of 1873, he embarrassed the government by his unauthorized use of some Post Office funds, he had to be removed to the Home Office, while Gladstone himself took over the exchequer for the remainder of his term.

Lowe then proceeded to boast of his record in hindering extravagance in government departments: "The first thing I did as Chancellor of the Exchequer was to issue an order that no new expenditure whatever would be allowed without my opinion first being taken upon it."[13] Such eagerness to keep the revenue under his own care in all details was no boon to the heads of the departments, who thus had an extra hurdle put in the way of their annual appropriations. Lowe's attitude on matters of administration at the British Museum varied from a Disraelian pride in outstanding acquisitions to a Gladstonian parsimony in regard to salaries. In 1874 he sat on a special committee of the trustees to study the question of printing the catalogue of accessions, and reported against the proposal. But he mellowed when out of office and helped the Museum staff to achieve a settlement with the treasury when negotiations seemed deadlocked in 1877.

In the Disraeli ministry from 1874 to 1880, the crucial time for the printing project, the chancellor of the exchequer was Sir Stafford Northcote, who had got his financial training at the Board of Trade under Gladstone when Gladstone was still a Conservative. It was Disraeli, however, who saw to Northcote's advancement to the posts of financial secretary to the treasury in 1859 and president of the Board of Trade in 1866. Northcote's name was indelibly connected with civil service reform, for in 1852 he had served on a commission to reorganize the Board of Trade, and from that beginning had gone on to investigate other departments with a view to their more efficient administration. He began his term of office in the Disraeli government by instituting an inquiry into what seemed to him the growing expense of the civil service in general. This was a worthwhile endeavor, yet it resulted in a painful chapter in the history of the British Museum when Northcote tried to force the administrative practices of that venerable institution into a pattern devised for one with more purely clerical staff.

Personally a gentle man, Northcote was ruled by a stern conscience. He also tended to be led by others and to cling stubbornly to his ideas, so that although he had the best intentions, his policies were often disliked and misinterpreted. As chancellor of the exchequer, despite his excellent financial background, he became the victim of world developments beyond his control. His logical concepts of budgeting were made inoperative by colonial wars and the great depression of the late seventies, so that having begun with a surplus of five millions bequeathed by Gladstone's administration, he was accused of having frittered it away when he ended his term with three years of deficit. In this frame of reference, Northcote's attempts to hold back salary reforms at the British Museum make a misguided kind of sense, but they were no less unpleasant to those who bore the brunt of his difficult rulings. Nevertheless, he allowed the printing of the accession titles by the Department of Printed Books, and for this Bond and Garnett were grateful.

Under the chancellor of the exchequer, the most important person at the treasury from the point of view of the British Museum was the financial secretary. He was responsible for the final form of the estimates of the next year's expenses sent in by the various departments, and for the adjustment of any difference of opinion between the treasury and the heads of the departments over those estimates. He also spoke for the Museum in Parliament, where all the money came from. Disraeli's choice for this important officer in 1874 was William Henry Smith, the railway "bookstall man," who, despite his background of "mere trade," had impressed his more respectable parliamentary peers by his amiable temperament and his integrity. Like Northcote, he was kindly, earnest, and devoted to duty. Disraeli wrote to him, "After forty years' experience in parliamentary life, I can only say that I never knew the affairs of the Treasury conducted with more thorough sense and efficiency than while they have been under your management and control."[14] He would seem to have been an ideal person for the principal librarian to deal with over the British Museum estimates.

Unfortunately, at the end of July 1877, the first lord of the admiralty died and Disraeli chose Smith to succeed him, an act which inspired one of the chief characters in Gilbert and Sullivan's *H.M.S. Pinafore*. The loss of Smith to the treasury came in the midst of the bargaining over a new salary scale for the British Musuem, and it resulted in a series of agonizing misunderstandings that ruined John Winter Jones's health. For, as Smith's replacement, Disraeli brought in the financial secretary to the War

Office, Sir Frederick Arthur Stanley, later sixteenth earl of Derby, who remained at the treasury for only nine months, after which he was made secretary for war. Stanley's lack of sympathy with such institutions as the British Museum hampered relations between the trustees and the treasury during an awkward period. In the spring of 1878 Stanley was followed in the financial secretaryship by Sir Henry Selwin-Ibbetson, who came there from the undersecretaryship of the Home Office. It was he who approved the initial grant for printing lists of accessions to the British Museum library.

At the head of the permanent staff of the treasury was the permanent secretary. His was the highest rank in the civil service, a position of great power, for all the political leaders had to look to him for information on financial affairs. From 1869 to 1885, under both parties, the incumbent was Ralph Robert Wheeler Lingen, a schoolfellow of Northcote's who had for twenty years before that been secretary to the Education Committee of the Privy Council. In 1859 Robert Lowe had become vice-president of this committee and the two men had begun a term of cooperation which came under severe censure in 1864. The basic complaint against them was their high-handed way of proceeding and their promotion of economy over every other consideration. A pair of efficiency experts, they were as ill liked as are most of their kind by more placid persons. The *Saturday Review* commented: "Mr. Lingen is quite as powerful [as Mr. Lowe] and a good deal more offensive. It is from Mr. Lingen that all the sharp snubbing replies proceed."[15] The officers of the British Museum were to receive their share of those harsh replies in 1877.

Lingen was reserved and strict and, being outside of politics, could afford to ignore the opinions of those who might be hurt by his fiscal intransigence. Yet he was businesslike and ran an efficient department, and he was anxious to spread good management throughout the civil service.

The Political Background

When in April 1880, the Liberals again took over the government, Prime Minister Gladstone once more acted as his own chancellor of the exchequer. Since the printing of catalogue entries for the British Museum library had been begun under the Conservatives, he could hardly fail to agree in December to the extension of the project to cover whole volumes of the catalogue. In May 1881, he resigned as a trustee of the Museum and in December 1882 he relinquished the chancellorship to H. C. E. Childers, who had learned finance from Gladstone as financial secretary to the treasury in the 1860s. Childers was so successful as chancellor that he nearly balanced the budget in 1884, and this was the year that publication of the entire British Museum catalogue of books was first funded by the treasury. Two financial secretaries facilitated the last two stages of the printing program: the ill-fated Lord Frederick Cavendish, murdered in Ireland in 1882; and Leonard Courtney, who left the treasury in 1884.

In June 1885, Childers's budget, inflated by a tax on beer to provide money for military preparedness vis-à-vis Russia, was defeated in the Commons and Gladstone resigned. The treasury also lost its long time watchdog, Lingen, who resigned and was made a peer. These two were succeeded by Lord Salisbury as prime minister and Reginald Earle Welby as permanent secretary to the treasury. Sir Michael Hicks Beach was chancellor of the exchequer, and though he brought in a period of financial retrenchment for the British Museum, the grant for printing the catalogue was so well established that it was accepted by the treasury as a normal expense. The brief return of Gladstone in 1886, followed by six years of Salisburian conservatism and the accompanying change-over of officials at the treasury had no effect on the printing funds, and the cataloguing engine produced a steady stream of printed entries until 1905, when the last supplementary volume came from the press.

Credit for support of the printing of the British Museum

catalogue, then, must be allotted equally to both political parties in an intensely partisan era. Disraeli, Northcote, and Selwin-Ibbetson were responsible for allowing the printing of accessions lists in 1879; Gladstone, Childers, Cavendish, and Courtney acceded to the second and third stages of the project in 1881 and 1884. Edward Bond was wise to take advantage of friendly leaders to inaugurate the printing program, for if it had not been moving along successfully, the Conservative government of the late 1880s might not have been so amenable to the increase of expenditure involved. The delicate task for all concerned was to strike a balance between the needs of the British Museum and the welfare of the nation.

IV. The Civil Service

When Panizzi persuaded the treasury to apply the regulations of the general civil service to the British Museum staff in 1857, in order that they might receive pensions, as other government workers did, he thereby began a connection from which he hoped much, but which was to have not altogether happy results. At first all went well, and, in addition to pensions, Panizzi in 1860 "extracted from an invariably reluctant Treasury considerable increases in salary and the creation of a new upper division to the grade of Assistant First Class, to which promotion would be by merit."[1] But for these concessions, he had to accept the rule establishing competitive examinations for vacant positions among three nominees, one of whom was to be chosen. Before long there resulted a poor appointment, for the civil service examinations had little to do with the kind of competence required in the library, and Panizzi, in his bellicose way, castigated the civil service commissioners for their method of selection. After an exchange of heated letters, the commissioners revenged themselves by refusing to approve any candidates for a Museum position. Although the Museum was later relieved of the requirement for the standard examinations, the atmosphere of discord thus begun was unfortunate for John Winter Jones to inherit as principal librarian, and he soon enough faced his own difficulties with the system.

Agitation for civil service reform had come to a peak in the early 1850s when the eighteenth-century custom of political patronage had begun to be seriously challenged. Parliament's main interest, however, was the same as that of the treasury—economy. An inquiry into the expense of the civil service establishment by a select committee of the House of Commons in 1848 had elicited the simplistic suggestion that the salaries of all civil servants be cut 10 percent. To this a strong rebuttal came in the testimony of Sir Charles Trevelyan, the assistant secretary to the treasury, who stated that public employees were over-worked and that a better solution would be a wiser use of manpower by relieving high-level officials of menial tasks.

The Northcote-Trevelyan Report

According to Disraeli,[2] it was a scandal in the Customs Office that forced Lord John Russell, when he was prime minister, to initiate a series of inquiries into several of the government departments which continued after the end of the Russell ministry in 1852. Trevelyan was on all the investigating committees and Sir Stafford Northcote was on eight of them. When the investigations were completed, Gladstone, the new chancellor of the exchequer, asked Northcote and Trevelyan to report on the prevailing situations in all the offices, with a view toward regularizing varying procedures. The result was the famous Northcote-Trevelyan Report of February 1854, entitled "Report on the Organization of the Permanent Civil Service," the fundamental document in all subsequent discussion and legislation on the subject. It advocated the separation of intellectual from mechanical work, the selection of clerks by open "competing literary examinations," and promotion as "the reward of merit."[3] These ideas aroused vigorous debate among politicians, while some unfortunate wording, designating the types of men who were likely to enter public service as "the unambitious and the indolent or incapable,"[4] caused hostility to the report among civil servants themselves. The application of the recommendations at that time would have amounted to a revolution in the conduct of public affairs for which the nation was not yet ready .

An untoward event provided an impetus toward the adoption of the Northcote-Trevelyan proposals. In March 1854, war was declared against Russia, and at first the British invasion of the Crimea went badly. The government was reluctant to believe the stories of the *Times* correspondent, who described bungling by the aristocratic generals and inefficiency in the system of supply, until statistical reports from its own representatives at the front provided confirmation. The Radicals, who had been against the war in the first place, stirred up public sentiment, and the *Times* rose to new heights of influence throughout Europe.

In 1855 there was a motion in the House of Commons to reform the army by abolishing the purchase of commissions and putting merit and competition in its stead. This, however, could not yet be done, for many army officers sat in Parliament, while the prime minister, Lord Palmerston, and the queen as well, opposed any interference with the army establishment. So the demand for military reform, especially after a few victories in the Crimea, was sublimated into widespread advocacy of administrative reform, "to destroy the aristocratic monopoly of power and place in the civil service."[5]

The tone of the debate became one of class against class, of "outs" versus "ins." Business leaders said that only those with the ability and drive necessary to mercantile activity would serve to replace the lackluster types, described by

Northcote and Trevelyan, who expected "an honourable livelihood with little labour and with no risk,"[6] and felt no shame for it. Such men caused, said the critics, bad government and public inconvenience, to say nothing of military incompetence.

Parliament, on the other hand, saw in the civil service a costly nuisance of increasing dimensions as the scope of public business grew after mid-century, and the cry went up to retrench on the extravagance of government offices. One of the specific targets was the overabundance of clerks at the higher levels of the service, many of whom were doing the same work as those receiving less pay. Another was the copying by hand of all communications: the Board of Trade had a copying press by 1850, but other offices were slow to acquire their own presses and the treasury before 1875 chiefly advocated making use of Her Majesty's Stationery Office for printing copies of reports and notices.

Gladstone was ever one of the staunchest supporters of open competition for civil service appointments: he considered it a good way to "open to the higly educated class . . . command over all the higher parts of the civil service"[7] which had formerly been staffed according to family and social status. Open competition was also favored by many Conservatives, including their leader, Lord Derby, and his lieutenant, Disraeli. But the only way to get the suggested examinations accepted by Prime Minister Palmerston was to stipulate that they were to be taken only by candidates nominated in the old way, through personal influence. A trio of civil service commissioners was chosen to judge and place the candidates. These mild measures had to be assimilated before stronger ones could be advanced.

The publicity and open discussion had, however, enabled comparisons among departments, and these had shown the civil servants that many of them deserved better salaries, working conditions, and opportunities for advancement. During the seventies the men began to protest these inequities in meetings and in the press. Gladstone managed to quiet the protests for a while by persuading the queen to issue two orders in council, the first of which permitted open competition for all vacancies in a selected group of offices on an experimental basis, and the second of which ordered that the temporary clerks called "writers," who were employed to copy reports and letters, were all to be examined by the Civil Service Commission.

These writers had banded together to form the Temporary Clerks and Civil Service Writers' Association, in order to press their claims. They held meetings which were fully reported in the *Times* and at which antagonism was freely expressed against Chancellor of the Exchequer Lowe. They knew that he wanted civil service reform only to save the nation money, not to benefit the civil servants themselves. By 1873 they were emboldened by support in Parliament to request a cost-of-living raise. The result of that was a select committee of the House of Commons, which reported in June, recommending that a commission be appointed by the crown to resurvey all the government departments, as a preliminary to covering legislation. Testimony before the committee had again suggested the use of copying machines to effect large savings on the salaries of writers.

The British Museum Staff

At the British Museum these activities stimulated latent ambitions. Although the staff had by then been largely exempted from civil service examinations, the treasury had been pressing the trustees to fill the ranks of junior assistants by open competition. The trustees, however, had declined, to the "regret"[8] of the lords commissioners. In April 1873, in response to memorials from various members of the staff, the trustees presented a scheme for raising all the salaries at the Museum, to which the treasury answered with "abruptness"[9] and in the negative.

Speeches were made in the Commons protesting such high-handed treatment of the respectable gentlemen of the Museum, but Lowe defended his decision, contending that the trustees had asked too much: the treasury never granted raises to a whole establishment at one time. Furthermore, the trustees had had the indiscretion to suggest the amount desired for increases, and to advise the staff of their recommendations before the treasury had had a chance to consider the request. Such irregularity, he said, took unfair advantage and could not be tolerated.

> Then it must be considered that the salaries at the British Museum were confessedly lower than in the Civil Service, and for obvious reasons. In the first place, instead of the drudgery of a clerk in an ordinary office, of the driest and most repulsive nature, very often spending whole days poring over figures, or transcribing, or indexing, these public servants were employed in a manner most delightful—that was, they were generally men of decided tastes for particular branches of science and learning, and they spent their time in a treasure house in which objects of art and antiquarian interest and books on every subject were collected together. They had the further advantage of a solid position somewhat higher than that of officials holding corresponding places in the Civil Service. It had always been assumed, therefore, that it was not necessary to give salaries quite on the scale of other offices.[10]

This rather heavy attempt at wit by the chancellor overlooked the fact that transcribing and indexing and cataloguing went on at the British Museum, and that the nature of all the work was much less idyllic than he would have his listeners believe. Lowe even insulted Principal Librarian Jones by saying that he hardly needed a raise because he was getting "the same salary as his excellent and deserving predecessor, Sir Antonio Panizzi," and he ended with a stab at the governing board:

> The Trustees had declined to accede to the suggestion of the Government to allow such places as the principle could properly be applied to, to be open to public competition. It was not unreasonable to ask those who wanted them to increase the salaries not only of the present officials, but of those coming after them, to show a willingness to adopt competition as being, in the opinion of Parliament, the best means of securing the services of the most efficient persons.[11]

The trustees understood that Lowe was for competition first and raises afterward, and they abandoned their request.

The Playfair Commission

Toward the end of the year the civil servants held a great meeting to adopt a petition to the chancellor of the exchequer for the alleviation of various grievances, but before any further action could be taken, Gladstone called for an election and his government fell. In February 1874, Disraeli at last regained the office he had held so briefly in 1868, and the new chancellor of the exchequer was the original investigator of the civil service, Sir Stafford Northcote. If the trustees of the British Museum seemed to have had enough trouble with Lowe, they had still more to look forward to with Northcote at the head of the treasury.

One of the new chancellor's first official deeds was to ask

Lyon Playfair to head a commission of inquiry on the expense of the civil service. Playfair, a chemist and professor at the School of Mines in London, had participated in many public investigations, beginning in the days of Robert Peel. He had sat in Parliament since 1868 for Edinburgh and St. Andrews universities and he showed some animosity toward the British Museum during the discussion of the educational appropriation for 1874. Arguing for a minister of education to exert effective control over education, science, and art, he deplored the concentration of museums and galleries in London: "They are suffering from a plethora of collections; their duplicates, their specimens, their redundant pictures, are packed away in boxes or are rotting in cellars; but if the provinces humbly sue even for a temporary loan from them, their deputations are sent away with the scantest courtesy."[12] This attack was unfair to the officers of the British Museum, who would have been glad of a solution to the overcrowding of their quarters, but were forbidden by their charter to lend except to a court of law, and then only so long as a member of the staff accompanied the article on loan.

With some reluctance Playfair consented to chair the commission; the other members were representatives of the higher levels of the civil service or members of Parliament. They at once began to take testimony, with a view to planning a reorganization that would meet all the needs of the various departments of government. The comprehensive report of this Civil Service Inquiry Commission, commonly known as the Playfair Commission, was turned in to the chancellor of the exchequer on December 24, 1874, and was subsequently sent to the heads of departments for their comments.

The recommendations of the commissioners stipulated that there should be a higher and a lower division of the service, based on education, with somewhat higher minimum and maximum salaries than had obtained before. Both ranks were to have the opportunity to earn extra "duty pay" for special services. The writers were to be admitted to the civil service as a separate third class and were to be paid as far as possible by piece work.[13] The commissioners also provided for attrition in the upper ranks for the lesser-paid employees, so that their work might be taken over by people in the lower ranks.

Northcote approved these ideas and pointed out in the Commons in 1876 that if a department proposed "bringing the scheme into operation in that Department and accompanied such proposals with a plan for re-organization, and, of course, reduction of the higher staff, the Treasury would be prepared to co-operate with the Department in such re-organization."[14] This was a warning of things to come for the British Museum, for it would be over this very point that much misunderstanding would arise in the following year. The plan dominated treasury thinking, but it was quite opposed to the situation and possibilities at the Museum, where Northcote tried to implement it.

V. The Treasury versus the British Museum

For several years the treasury had kept up a steady pressure on the officers of the British Museum to save on paper and copying costs. On April 8, 1872, for example, the heads of the departments were sent the following letter by the principal librarian:

> The Lords Commissioners of the Treasury have requested the Trustees to furnish to the Stationery Office a statement of the amount which may be fairly taken as the cost of the clerical labour expended on each document presented to Parliament in order that it may be shewn in conjunction with the cost of Printing &c; this statement to include not only any extra clerical labour which may be found necessary, but also the estimated cost of ordinary clerical labour used to prepare such documents.
>
> Will you be so good as to send me a statement accordingly with reference to clerical labour bestowed upon the account of Progress now in course of preparation for Parlt.[1]

Keeper Rye penciled at the top of his copy, "spoke to Mr.

J[ones] respecting this," as though he felt there was more behind the request than was immediately apparent. One assistant reported that he spent three-quarters of an hour on his portion of the account, the cost to the treasury being about one shilling.[2]

In November the principal librarian had to ask his heads of departments for more statistics:

> The Treasury having directed that, in the preparation of the Estimates for the coming financial year, all payments of the nature of "personal remuneration" which it may be proposed to make, shall be provided for under the sub-head of "Salaries and Wages," I shall be glad to receive from you, on or before Saturday next, the 23rd Inst., a statement as to what portion of the amount you recommend to be provided for catalogues, &c. for your Department will be paid by way of personal remuneration to persons engaged or to be engaged on the catalogues; and what portion to tradesmen for printing, &c. &c.
>
> You will please to give full details in reference to the personal remuneration.[3]

Jones soon afterward produced a report on the positions of all the employees of the Museum to satisfy the curiosity of the treasury as to whether their wish that the assistants should not be paid extra for "ordinary duties," even in overtime, was being adhered to.

With the change in government in 1874 a fresh attempt was made by the staff of the Museum to better its situation. On April 13, the assistants drew up a memorial requesting salary increases, and, on June 17, through the recommendation of a special subcommittee on which Robert Lowe sat, three keepers and the lower class of assistants were given raises. This small victory occasioned protests by the first-class assistants, who claimed to be discriminated against, as they would not have been according to the arrangements devised by the trustees and rejected by the treasury the previous year.

The Second Civil Service Inquiry

In April 1875, Lyon Playfair and four others were appointed to try to apply the recommendations of the Civil Service Inquiry Commission to each of the public departments. This was, in fact, to move on to another of the subjects of the inquiry as first set up: "The appointments in various offices requiring special and technical qualifications, and in such establishments as the British Museum and the Department of Science and Art."[4] The report on this topic, the "Second Report of the Civil Service Inquiry Commission," is dated May 14, 1875, and was of vital concern to the British Museum.

The Museum's part of the report was based on evidence taken from Jones and two members of the library staff, as well as representatives of the other departments. Statements were handed in for the senior and junior assistants, the officers, and the minority opinion among the keepers and assistant keepers, who sent their own representative to speak against open competition for vacancies. Jones then made a separate appearance to comment on the evidence given by the employees. He defended the system of patronage at the Museum on the basis of its being written into the law which had established the institution, the power of appointment being vested in the three principal trustees. The standing committee of the trustees had suggested that these three should nominate a group of men who would then compete by examination for vacant positions. Jones claimed that promotions were made according to merit, although the assistants contended that seniority was usually the deciding factor. In actuality, any promotion of a junior over a senior employee caused ill feeling, whereas promotion by seniority was seldom questioned.

There were twenty-eight junior assistants in the Museum, and their work was far from menial, although much of it was tedious. The fifteen junior assistants in the Department of Printed Books, who copied out the entries for the catalogue, shared among themselves enough knowledge of all major languages and alphabets to be able to decipher accurately the handwriting of the senior assistants on the title slips. They also incorporated the slips into the volumes of the catalogue.

The senior assistants were divided into an upper and a lower section, according to length of service, and there were sixteen men in the upper and forty-three in the lower section. Their work was regulatory, advisory, and supervisory. The thirteen in Printed Books did the original cataloguing, the arranging of the books on the shelves, and the revision of the work of the juniors, and they were responsible for the service in the reading room.

All three of these groups felt aggrieved in regard to salaries. The first report of the Playfair Commission had opened their eyes to the situation in other branches of the civil service, while Lowe's comments in the House of Commons had shown them that their lower remuneration was considered in some quarters to be compensated for by the loftiness of their pursuits. The second Playfair commission acknowledged the discrepancy in Museum wages compared to those in the rest of the service, but could only offer as a remedy the continued use of duty pay for special tasks outside Museum hours. The testimony of the investigation made it clear that a reorganization of the staff levels at the Museum would be healthy, since the present system was discriminatory in several ways. The commissioners did not deem it expedient to adopt open competition, but thought that appointments would best be made "on the joint responsibility of the head of the department, the Lords of the Treasury, and the Civil Service Commissioners."[5] The interjection of the latter two bodies into the appointment process constituted an unwelcome impediment to the traditional policy.

Printing Suggested

Equally unwelcome was the Playfair recommendation that ordinary civil service clerks be brought in to do some of the work of the junior assistants. However, a paragraph on this subject included words which started the long chain of events that led to the publication of the general catalogue:

> We are of opinion that these institutions [the British Museum and the South Kensington, now the Victoria and Albert, Museum] should be organized in such a manner and with such a scale of remuneration, as would attract to them men of high literary, artistic, and scientific culture. The present arrangements for the employment of the junior officers in the Library of the British Museum might with advantage be reconsidered; and if a staff corresponding to the Lower Division of the General Civil Service were introduced into the Museum, *and printing instead of transcribing were freely resorted to* [italics mine], a considerable saving of expense would probably be effected, which would meet the increased cost of a small number of well paid officers of the higher grades.[6]

On October 6, the new keeper of printed books, George Bullen, drew up a report giving his opinion of the proposal to use printing for the sake of economy:

> Mr Bullen, presuming that this suggestion refers mainly to the compilation of the Catalogues, begs to

state that, having investigated the subject carefully, he is of opinion that no pecuniary saving whatever would be effected by printing instead of transcribing the slips from which the Catalogue is compiled. Indeed the expense of printing would exceed that of transcription by more than one half.

Moreover, even if printing were less expensive than transcribing (which is not the case), it would be very inexpedient to have recourse to it now, after the Catalogue has been transcribed to the end of letter R. There remain only certain titles in the letters S to Z to be transcribed: and when these shall have been completed, it will be a proper time, Mr Bullen thinks, to take into consideration the great question of printing the greatest Catalogue in the world—that of the Library of the British Museum.

At present, to print the slips of the remaining letters of the Alphabet would lead only to disturbance and confusion, while no advantage, that Mr Bullen can see, would be gained.

The great object of printing a Catalogue is, of course, to multiply copies. Now, had the Catalogue been commenced on this principle, a great deal might be said in favour of printing, on the ground that various minor catalogues might be formed, and a Classified Index constructed, with the aid of the numerous copies that might be struck off in the printing. All this would have been very expensive, but there would have been corresponding advantages, were the entire Catalogue so printed. In printing the slips, however, from S to Z this would not be the case. We do not require to multiply copies of the entries in those letters, while we have only four copies in all the other letters; any greater number of copies would be of no use to us; and the estimates would be saddled with twice the expense. Mr Bullen is, therefore, decidedly in favour of continuing the present system of transcribing the titles in preference to printing them, until the entire Catalogue from A to Z shall have been completed.[7]

Bullen never changed these sentiments, but clung stubbornly to his determination to postpone printing until the manuscript catalogue was finished. Unfortunately, although there were only a few letters left, there were many, many entries in those letters. Bullen projected the end of the transcribing and revision in seven years, which proved to be fairly accurate, and this did not seem to him too long to wait in order to have a more perfect catalogue when it was committed to type. Moreover, his reluctance to embrace the "disturbance and confusion" of a new process introduced among the routines so long established is understandable from an administrative point of view. Yet his stance amounted to obstructionism in the eyes of those who felt more keenly the forces impelling the department toward print.

Reorganization Plans

The work of the Civil Service Inquiry Commission had given the staff an impetus toward bettering their condition, and it had also given the treasury a goal for the reform of the departmental structure. These factors, coinciding with the preparations for the transfer of the natural history collections to a new building on the South Kensington site, resulted in an attempt to reorganize the entire establishment during 1877.

Just a year after the second report of the commission, that is, on April 24, 1876, a question was asked in the House of Commons as to whether, in the light of the commissioners' comment on the smallness of the salaries at the Museum, the government had any plan to remedy the situation. Financial Secretary W. H. Smith replied that "owing to the prolonged consideration of the First Report of the Civil Service Inquiry Commission the attention of the Government had not yet been given to the Second Report . . . [but] that the matter would be duly considered."[8] The officers of the Museum had, however, decided to take matters into their own hands. On May 3, Winter Jones submitted to the treasury, with a covering letter of explanation and support, memorials from the keepers, the assistant keepers, the accountant, and the senior assistants of the upper section, all requesting raises.

No direct answer was made to this proposal, and on July 3 in the House a question was asked of the chancellor of the exchequer, whether the government had received any recommendation from the trustees of the Museum in regard to salaries, and if so, what answer had been returned. Northcote replied:

> Sir, the Treasury have received a request from the trustees of the British Museum to inquire into the position of the officers of that Department, with a view to a revision both of their salaries and of their duties. All I can say on the subject at present is that the recommendations will be considered, and that we hope to be able to make a satisfactory explanation before the next Estimates are prepared.[9]

Before time for the estimates of the next year's budget, however, in August, when the final vote of money for the current year came before the House, it was pointed out by a member that "there was a long-standing grievance on the part of the officials of the British Museum which had now been under consideration since the year 1836," and that the staff had been enlarged threefold in that time, in fact, "everything had been increased but the amount of remuneration."[10] Spencer Walpole, a devoted trustee, reminded the House that after the report of the Playfair Commission "the Treasury in the case of the British Museum reserved to itself the power of considering in what way the officers and assistants in that institution should be appointed and paid under the new regulations."[11] Therefore Parliament's hands were tied. The House proceeded to vote the Museum's appropriation for the rest of the year, but the treasury was not inspired to hurry its consideration of the salary question.

At last, on February 2, 1877, a long letter setting forth the treasury position was sent over Lingen's signature. It conveyed the treasury's agreement to raises for the keepers and assistant keepers, but not for the assistants, as the upper division of the "Playfair Scale" of remuneration was thought to be adequate for them. Furthermore, a condition was imposed: that the assistants be chosen by competition among three applicants for each position, their examinations to involve special areas of knowledge to suit special jobs. A probationary period of six months was stipulated, but that was already Museum practice. Most threatening was the request that the trustees consider whether all thirteen departments, each under a keeper at top salary, were really necessary; and the letter ended with an overt warning: "My Lords would not be disposed to agree to any such change as this unless it were accepted as a settlement which should put an end to further applications, except for increase of numbers, for many years to come."[12]

The trustees mulled over the treasury proposals and replied in April that they could agree to some of them, but that the Playfair scale was unfair to the best senior assistants of the lower section, who would be set back, rather than advanced as they deserved to be. It would seem wise to amalgamate the four sections of assistants into two, senior and junior. Lingen's answer was that he would prefer only one class, which would fit the Playfair scheme: duty pay could be depended upon to make up for distinction by merit. However, the chancellor of the exchequer was now "willing to meet a small Committee of the Trustees in order to discuss verbally the points which remain unsettled."[13] The trustees approved the idea of a high-level conference, and suggested that it be held at the British Museum, where the papers needed would be readily available. Lingen replied that the chancellor was much too busy to come to the Museum.

The trustees, therefore, went to Downing Street, a place not unfamiliar to Robert Lowe and the duke of Somerset, who were the delegated conferees. Their meeting, on July 19, 1877, resulted in a plan for reorganization that avoided the more cramping recommendations of the Playfair Commission report, although Lingen reiterated his plea that the higher rank of assistants be decreased in number and that printing be used to effect economy in the overall budget. Jones, in turn, protested that the salaries thus agreed to were still not equitable and that decreasing the total number of employees would be disastrous.

Indeed, there were a number of vacancies to be filled throughout the Museum, five of them in the Department of Printed Books, where the transcription of titles for the catalogue was so delayed that two assistants had been assigned to help out the transcribers. This arrangement held back the original cataloguing of accessions. Yet the treasury turned a deaf ear to all requests for more rather than less staff, and the trustees, caught in a cross-fire between the officers and the men who controlled the Museum funds, decided to placate the latter. On October 13, the standing committee resolved: "That the Trustees declined to make any further demands upon the Treasury."[14]

A subsequent exchange of letters resulted in an acceptable, if not entirely satisfactory, resolution of the last debated items, and Jones was able to prepare the estimates for the coming year before the middle of December. Then he escaped to Cornwall to recuperate from the strain of the negotiations.

The *Athenaeum* published three sarcastic notices of the "much-vexed" salary question at the British Museum, remarking in June of 1877 that when it was settled

> it may even prove possible to complete the catalogue of the magnificent collection of printed books, a catalogue which, after occupying an immense staff more than thirty years, has reached only the letter S, and is, as yet, unprovided with any sort of index. The economists, who object to paying fair salaries to the scholars they employ, will be astonished if they ever learn what the as yet unfinished catalogue has cost the nation. [15]

To the scholars who have relied on it, Panizzi's "New General Catalogue" has been worth every penny, but there is no doubt that the savings possible from the adoption of print for the entries were already, by 1878, long overdue.

Copyists in the British Museum

During Jones's holiday, Charles Newton substituted for him as acting principal librarian, and at his first meeting with the trustees in this capacity, he presented a letter from the treasury approving the estimates for 1878-79, but stating that

> they would be glad to see the experiment of employing the Assistants, out of office hours, in piece work, extended to the Index of Printed Books, their Lordships believing that the payment at the rate of ¼d. per index-slip, as a maximum such as had been authorized for the index to the Charters would be

found much cheaper and to ensure much greater rapidity of work than the system of employing purely salaried labour.[16]

This had been Edward Bond's solution to the problem of getting money to finance the compilation of indexes to the charters and rolls in the Department of Manuscripts, and his experiment was thought to indicate the feasibility of applying the system to the Department of Printed Books' catalogue, which apparently was meant by the term "Index of Printed Books." Work on catalogues was often done outside of regular hours, but the general catalogue was so enormous that it required full-time staff in the Museum as well as extra work outside it.

The question was referred to the subcommittee on printed books and manuscripts, which consisted of Somerset, Walpole, and Lowe. When they met on February 25, Newton put before them an alternative suggestion from Bullen that

> as an experiment, seven copyists should be obtained for six months, the selection of the men to be left to the Keeper of Printed Books . . . and a report to be submitted to the Trustees upon the work of the copyists at the end of six months. . . .[17]

The subcommittee agreed to the hiring of these "copyists," as the civil service writers were now called, to transcribe "ordinary" entries for the catalogue at a lower rate of pay, while the assistants were to continue the copying of difficult titles. Unfortunately, although their trial period was twice extended, the copyists proved to be so deficient in foreign languages that their transcribing, said Bullen, "causes the introduction of numerous errors into the entries and impedes the progress of the Catalogue."[18] The solution was to "give notice" to the worst offenders and to ask the civil service commissioners for more linguistically sophisticated men to replace them at the same low wage.

Machines Proposed

Another scheme of the Northcote treasury was to promote the introduction of mechanical means of copying wherever possible in the government offices. However, the machines available were so inefficient that their use was resisted by such specialized establishments as the British Museum. In the spring of 1878 an investigation was made by a committee headed by one of the treasury officials, Rowland Winn, into the possibilities for mechanization. The copying work of all the departments, the committee decided, would best be concentrated into one specific branch of each department, then eventually into one Division of Copying for the entire civil service. Meanwhile, the copying of official letters should be expedited by the application of either the Fellows process or the typewriter.

The Fellows process involved a special thick ink and specially prepared paper to act as a matrix from which an impression could be taken by placing the sheet in a press for half a minute, for up to six copies, or somewhat longer for more copies. The typewriter was an outgrowth of several inventions in England, France, and the United States, and although it was in 1878 that bars with two sizes of type were introduced, the machines under consideration at the British Museum in that year had only uppercase letters. Winn's committee announced that the controller of Her Majesty's Stationery Office was prepared to provide the materials for the Fellows process and to loan typewriters, while both systems might be seen in operation at the Post Office and at the Board of Inland Revenue.

In response to these suggestions Bullen expressed his objections to the typewriter as totally inadequate, in its then state of development, for making catalogue entries, and rejected the Fellows process, so far as he could "understand it from the description given"[19] in a treasury circular of March 25, as less convenient than the method of carbon copying customary in the Department of Printed Books. Finally, in May of 1878, Jones submitted a report on all the suggestions so far given, and at a meeting on the first of June the subcommittee on printed books and manuscripts considered everything and reported to the standing committee that the mechanical arrangements promoted by the treasury were not, in their opinion, applicable to the work of the British Museum.

Thus were lines of conflict drawn between the Museum and the treasury, each side considering the other uncooperative and stubborn. The Museum needed more staff for its increasing business; the treasury wanted it to do with less. The trustees liked their private way of selecting employees; the treasury wanted to broaden it. To the trustees, the entire staff was underpaid; to the treasury it was paid quite well enough for the kind of work in which it was engaged. To the treasury, any copyist should be able to produce acceptable catalogue entries; to the officials of the Department of Printed Books, very special qualifications were necessary in such personnel. To the treasury, machines seemed to offer a cure-all; to the Museum officers, the available machines were too imperfect to be of use. These divergences would be far from easy to reconcile: a master negotiator was called for.

VI. The Catalogue of Early English Books

Several special catalogues were being compiled in the Department of Printed Books during the 1870s. Each of them had to be authorized and financed separately, outside regular departmental funds; but there was seldom any question about them because their compass and cost were small compared to the general catalogue, and specialized catalogues appealed to educated men such as those who sat on the board of trustees and those who staffed the treasury. In 1871 was published W. B. Rye's catalogue of the remainder of the Grenville library which had not been included in the Payne and Foss catalogue of 1842-1884. In 1874 the treasury approved an offer by Trübner to publish at a favorable price a catalogue of the Sanskrit books, which was completed in 1876. Robert Kennaway Douglas, the orientalist, finished his catalogue of the Chinese books in 1877 and started one of the Japanese books, while T. W. Lidderdale catalogued the Icelandic collections. And all the time the department supported the compilation of separate catalogues of maps and music.

It was another special catalogue, however, that took the spotlight away from the general catalogue at a time when the pressure to print it, from both outside and inside the Museum, was mounting. The conception of the *Catalogue of Books in the Library of the British Museum Printed in England, Scotland, and Ireland, and of Books in English Printed Abroad, to the Year 1640*, as it gained favor during these same years, can be traced to the journalist Charles Wentworth Dilke, who had edited the *Athenaeum* from 1830 to 1845 and later wrote for it. Dilke had once been librarian to the House of Lords and took a great interest in library matters. A series of articles in the *Athenaeum* in 1850,[1] which are generally attributed to him, reviewed the report of the Royal Commission on the British Museum. In them he strongly advocated, first, the printing of a "finding" or short-title catalogue of the Museum library, and then the compilation of a universal catalogue.

In between these two proposals fell what would become, according to his plan, the British section of the latter, a catalogue of all books published in the English language or printed in the British territories. The British Museum's general catalogue of printed books would provide many of these titles, but for those not held by the Museum library, he suggested that Panizzi, while completing his own catalogue, should hire "additional assistants, one, two, or three, as may be desired, who shall, under his direction, consult libraries, catalogues, and bibliographical works,"[2] and prepare the entries for a complete catalogue of British printing since it began. Panizzi's reaction to this well-meant, but impossible, proposal can well be imagined, considering all the tasks his staff was already burdened with, and the reluctance of the trustees and the treasury to authorize funds for more staff for any reason.

The Society of Arts

Such a utopian attitude marked most of the rhetoric about the universal catalogue at that period. The promoters' concept was of a short-title list printed on cheap paper in tiny type, like a dictionary or a public document, and a sample of this sort was prepared by Sir Henry Cole of the Society of Arts. He had taken up the advocacy of Dilke's plan in 1852, but at that time the suggestion was premature, and only in 1875 did it seem feasible to try it again. Then Cole had some sheets of entries printed to show that his idea "was not necessarily impracticably vague."[3] He presented these to the Prince of Wales, hoping for sponsorship, and three years later the prince, as president of the Society of Arts, asked that its council look into "the cost of producing a catalogue of all the books printed in the United Kingdom up to 1600, and the plan of a universal catalogue of which that might be a part."[4]

The council held a series of hearings at which prominent librarians and literary men were asked to give their opinions. The English catalogue was the dominant topic, since it would precede the universal catalogue, and since of the two, it was the easier of attainment. All those involved assumed that the British Museum library would provide the basis for the early English catalogue, with the Department of Printed Books being responsible for the compilation, as so large a part of the work had already been done there in making the title slips for the general catalogue. It was expected that the Bodleian, the Cambridge University Library, and the other major libraries of the United Kingdom would contribute entries which the British Museum staff would intercalate with their own. The government would then have the whole printed at the Stationery Office. Bullen testified in favor of an early English catalogue of the holdings of the British Museum alone, but not of the cooperative venture.

Henry Bradshaw's Contribution

Quite a different sort of person had a part in the decision

to compile this catalogue: the bibliographer and expert on early printing, Henry Bradshaw of Cambridge University, whose interest in the matter came from his own research needs. He wanted a printed list of the incunabula in the British Museum library, which he called "that most hopeless of all places"[5] for finding examples of books from specific early presses, because they were entered only by author in the catalogue, and he thought they should also be cross-referenced to the locations where they had been printed. In April 1871, Bradshaw had written to Winter Jones to request that a staff member be assigned to make up such a list. He even proposed a person who would do the job well, J. H. Hessels, who had been working with Bradshaw for several years and was thoroughly trained in Bradshaw's method of investigating early printing. Jones replied that there was, regrettably, no vacancy on the staff of the Department of Printed Books which Hessels could fill, nor could he relieve any other assistant of his regular duties in order to work on such a list.

The following year Bradshaw found an opportunity to reopen the negotiations through Spencer Walpole, member of Parliament for Cambridge University and one of the most active trustees of the British Museum. Walpole suggested that a memorial be presented to the trustees setting forth the value of a catalogue of the works of the earliest English printers held by the British library. Such a memorial was duly drafted by Hessels, approved by Bradshaw, and signed by eight eminent literary men. It was referred by the trustees to Jones and by him to Keeper Rye, who reported his opinion on May 9, 1872. The projected work would, he said, "rather constitute a bibliographical work than a Catalogue in the proper sense of the word,"[6] and he expressed doubt that it should be given preference over other possible uses of department time and money. His view prevailed, and Bradshaw's efforts thus came to naught.

After having made his unfavorable report on the Bradshaw proposal, however, Rye had proceeded to prepare for the day when the trustees might feel inclined to take up the matter again. In 1875, as he was about to retire, he wrote a report on the state of his department in which he said that the title slips of all the fifteenth-century books and of English books printed before 1640 "have been separated from the great bulk of titles, and are under the charge of the Attendant Vincent," so that "special catalogues, either printed or manuscript, if considered advisable, might be formed."[7] Eventually, Bullen was able to make good use of these slips.

The Library Association

The founding of the Library Association of the United Kingdom in the fall of 1877 provided another opportunity to air the need for catalogues of all kinds. At the initial meeting, the universal catalogue, the early English catalogue, and a printed catalogue of the British Museum library were all discussed. W. E. A. Axon repeated the sentiment of the Royal Commission of 1850 that the latter venture would raise the cultural level of the nation and would be essential to the fulfillment of the Museum's role as a national institution. George Bullen agreed that a printed catalogue would be useful and thought a total cost of £100,000 was not exorbitant if it were extended over ten years. It would be "repaid by possession of the best catalogue the world ever saw."[8] Russell Martineau, an assistant in the Department of Printed Books who was expert both in cataloguing and in early printing, was on the opposite side, reiterating the old objection that a printed catalogue was "obsolete immediately,"[9] and pointing out the high potentiality for errors in cataloguing older works, errors which were easy to correct in manuscript, but difficult once they were in print.

John Winter Jones, in the chair, expressed his doubts about the feasibility of a printed catalogue for the British Museum library, agreeing with Martineau that such a catalogue would never be current. He also felt that without classification the usefulness of the work would be greatly impaired. Both Bullen and Richard Garnett agreed that a subject catalogue would be highly desirable and easier of achievement than the alphabetical catalogue, since the fourth slips of entries were already filed in shelf order and thus roughly by subject. Garnett also said that in regard to the alphabetical author catalogue, he was "averse to attempting to print it just as it stands . . . because I regard the undertaking as beyond our strength."[10] He would prefer to print a subject catalogue in sections, as he was sure they "would by their sale nearly repay the expense of publication, which a complete alphabetical catalogue of the library would not."[11]

By a "subject catalogue" in this context Garnett must have meant the printing of special headings in the main catalogue which comprised subject or author bibliographies, for a year later he was an advocate of printing the whole general catalogue, beginning with special headings. On the other hand, although Bullen said in 1878 that "it was his firm desire to have a complete catalogue printed of the contents of the British Museum [library],"[12] he was not at all ready for the project when Bond and Garnett were.

Instead, he favored the idea which Cornelius Walford expressed when he urged the Library Association to undertake "A New General Catalogue of English Litera-ture."[13] Edward Arber had, a few months before, announced that he was "now solving the question of English printed bibliography down to 1660 A.D."[14] by having printed, at his own expense, the *Stationers' Registers* to 1640, and by beginning to compile a bibliography of all English and colonial printing to 1660 which would be issued in annual lists. This noble work was not, however, accepted by his peers as supplanting the aspirations of Walford. For Walford had in mind a union catalogue of holdings in all the libraries and the private collections of the kingdom, to be financed by a government grant and headed by a popular author, and to be compiled by means of form slips that would be filled out in the various institutions and private collections by their staffs or owners. If this scheme proved not to be feasible, an officer of the Library Association could, Walford thought, go around to all these libraries and catalogue all the books he could find that fitted the category.

These impossible ideas were actually taken seriously by the council of the association, and an eleven-member committee was subsequently appointed which met monthly to trade opinions on the different aspects of the project. Bullen was a member of the committee, but seems not to have attended the meetings.

Finally, at the meeting of July 1878, the committee resolved that the joint secretaries of the association, Henry R. Tedder and Ernest C. Thomas, "communicate with the Museum authorities."[15] They wrote a letter to the principal librarian, Winter Jones, who was also the president of the Library Association, describing the proposal as so far agreed upon—an alphabetical author catalogue with subject indexes—and said:

If a complete printed Catalogue of the British Museum were in existence (and more especially one of the English books) the work of any society commencing a General Catalogue would be much simplified, and the Committee learn with great satisfaction that it is under consideration to partially remedy the want of a Catalogue of English Books down to 1640. As under any circumstances the riches of the British Museum must form the basis of a General Catalogue, they were of opinion that it would be highly undesirable to do so much of the work twice over, and they resolved in consequence:

"That the authorities of the British Museum be urged to make their proposed Catalogue of English Books down to 1640 cover the whole existing printed literature of the period, and not confine it to a list of the books in one library."

We have therefore the honour to ask the Trustees of the British Museum favorably to consider this suggestion. Should they decide to do so, the Council of the Library Association would undertake to use their organization for the supply of additional slips, prepared by librarians and private collectors on a uniform system, and thus supplementing the collection of the British Museum to insure an authoritative Catalogue of the whole of English literature down to 1640.[16]

The secretaries also offered an alternative: that the association would be responsible for the compiling of the catalogue if the British Museum library would supply title slips for all its English books.

The reply to these rather presumptuous suggestions was unceremoniously short and blunt:

Gentlemen: I have had the honour to lay before the Trustees of the British Museum the letter which, on the part of the Library Association of the United Kingdom, you addressed to me on the 12th ult; and I have been directed to acquaint you, for the information of the Library Association, that the Trustees feel that they must decline to take any part in the preparation of a General Catalogue of English Literature.

I have the honour to be, gentlemen, Your obedient servant, J. Winter Jones, Principal Librarian.[17]

On the same day that this letter was penned, the committee met again and "resolved to draw up a code of rules for compiling the proposed catalogue, based upon those of the British Museum, of Mr. [Charles Ammi] Cutter, and of the [American Library Association]."[18] Undaunted by the trustees' rebuff, they continued to meet and to plan, and they received a good deal of support when they reported to the annual meeting of the Library Association at Oxford the following October. Richard Garnett, in a sarcastic paragraph on this meeting, described the occasion thus:

If ridicule could kill, [the proposal] could hardly have survived the discussion which arose among its advocates at the late Oxford Conference. Those external to the Museum suggested that the Museum should catalogue not only the old English books it possessed, but also those it did not possess. The Museum representatives [Bullen and Garnett], enamoured with the project as they were, pleaded that it would be unreasonable to expect them to describe what they had never seen. The other side concurred, but represented in turn that a catalogue of such English books only as happened to be in a particular library would be very imperfect, and of very little use. Having thus mutually demonstrated the unreasonableness of the proposal from one point of view, and its inutility from another, they agreed that it should by all means be persevered with, and went home.[19]

Garnett's object was by then to get the Museum's general catalogue of books in all languages into print as speedily as possible, and he was strongly against the evasion of this necessary activity by employing "money and labour in telling a few specialists what they already know."[20] He considered frivolous the idea of publishing "a catalogue of English books before 1641, or just the period when books were beginning to be useful,"[21] noting that the cutoff year was chosen to avoid the huge mass of English revolutionary tracts in the Thomason collection, "a special catalogue of which would be really valuable."[22] Garnett was pretty much alone in his sentiments, however. Most of the enthusiasts in England wanted an early English catalogue to be compiled, no matter by whom.

The Trustees Decide

In the meantime the trustees had been reacting to the continued pressure from the public, the Library Association, and the treasury to expedite the work on the manuscript general catalogue of printed books. All the parties agreed that the transcribing should be speeded up, but so much had been said about printing that the feasibility of applying that method to the catalogue must now be reconsidered. The treasury letter of January 12, 1878, which had requested the employment of assistants in extra time to decrease the backlog of titles awaiting transcription, had started the movement toward a new approach to the catalogue problem. The deliberations of the library sub-committee had resulted in the initiation, not of a piecework system, but of an experimental hiring of copyists for the job. The subcommittee had also seen a letter from Garnett "offering suggestions for printing the Catalogue; with notes by Mr. Bullen,"[23] and a letter to Garnett from the Advocates' Library, Edinburgh, revealing the costs involved in their recently adopted catalogue-printing program.

What Bullen's comments on Garnett's suggestions may have been, we do not know; but the subcommittee followed his expressed desires rather than Garnett's when they ended their report by saying:

With reference to the question of Printing any part of the Catalogue of Printed Books, your Sub-Committee have directed the Keeper to report on the expediency of printing a catalogue of English books from the invention of printing up to the year 1640, or a catalogue of any one class of books, such as those entered under the headings 'Bible,' 'Liturgies,' 'Shakspere,' and 'Periodical Publications,' etc.[24]

The idea of printing such special headings had long been bandied about, but the usual objection—the incompleteness of the manuscript catalogue—had always been raised to end the discussion. The staff, the trustees, and the treasury were all aware that the volumes of the larger headings in the reading room catalogue were becoming impossibly unwieldy, "those gorged ones that readers know so well, of original width at the back, but swelling to double breadth in the middle through additional entries."[25] The subcommittee had named the very largest headings, but there were a number of others which also needed to be printed to gain space for shelving the catalogue and to ease the problem of handling the volumes for the patrons.

When Bullen submitted his report on March 7, however, he made the astonishing statement that

there is still sufficient space for some years for the growth and accommodation of the Catalogue in the Reading Room, and that, in any case, the relief to be obtained by the printing of such headings would be inconsiderable. Mr. Bullen cannot, therefore, recommend the printing of any of these headings separately at present.[26]

Thus did he dispose of Garnett's chief argument for print. He continued by recommending the compilation of the early English catalogue:

The title-slips for the English books up to the year 1640 have already been selected . . . and placed in boxes apart. They would, however, require a careful revision, and perhaps some additions to make them suitable for a special bibliographical catalogue such as might satisfy critics in the present advanced state of bibliographical science. For example, the names of printers and publishers in every instance ought to be mentioned.... Collations and bibliographical notes would also have to be supplied in numerous instances.[27]

Therefore, although a large part of the work appeared to have been done, a great deal more still remained, in Bullen's opinion, if the catalogue were to please such experts as Bradshaw. But upon this recommendation the trustees ordered:

> That Mr. Bullen be directed to prepare, as soon as he is enabled to do so, the materials for a Catalogue of all the English books in the Museum Library issued from the introduction of printing to the year 1640. That Mr. Bullen report to the Trustees as soon as the proposed Catalogue shall be in a proper state to be sent to press.[28]

So still another catalogue was authorized to be produced by the Department of Printed Books along with all its other duties and while the many problems occasioned by the bulk of the general catalogue continued unabated.

Bullen's Catalogue

The work on the early English catalogue got under way, but it proceeded at a leisurely pace. In May 1881, Bullen made a premature report to the trustees of its completion. He said it contained "about 25,000 entries, including main-titles and cross-references. These are now revised and almost ready to be sent to Press...."[29] He anticipated that it would run to three volumes octavo and requested permission to get a sample sheet from the printer. Then he added that the work should have two indexes, one of subjects and one of printers and publishers, indicating that Bradshaw's hope for this feature was going to be fulfilled. Bullen suggested that the assistant who had been revising the entries be hired to make the indexes at home and be paid by the slip.

In October of 1881 Bullen was able to project publication during the next fiscal year and requested that a sum be put in the estimates to cover the printing. The best bid was from William Clowes and Sons, the future printers of the general catalogue, and was computed for either 500 or 1,000 copies. The trustees settled for 750 copies and asked the treasury for £600, which was allowed,[30]

In 1882, however, this whole process was gone through again, Clowes submitting the lowest bid on July 4.[31] Then real results ensued, for in his annual report of the Department of Printed Books, Bullen announced that volume 1 of the catalogue of early English books was in print, and in June 1884, the third and last volume was presented to the trustees.[32]

The reception by the literary world of this long-anticipated work was tepid. The *Athenaeum* said that its "well-drafted scheme," "abundant cross references and good indexes" made it "positive bibliography," and went on:

> Naturally this first edition exhibits some defects. It has, therefore, been wisely limited to about seven hundred copies for sale, and it is not unlikely that, instead of supplements, a new and enlarged edition will before long be called for....[33]

Noting that "these three volumes cannot contain much more than one-half of the whole body of English literature in existence prior to 1640," the writer nevertheless stated that "all parties concerned are entitled to the best thanks of English readers all over the world."

In the *Academy*, W. E. A. Axon "cordially commended" the work as "well-printed," "drawn with care," and to be accepted

> both as a valuable addition to bibliographical literature and as a welcome indication of the present policy of the Museum authorities. If they can exercise sufficient patience, the various schools of bibliographers and the various classes of students may hope to have their [catalogue] needs supplied.[34]

There is no doubt that Bullen's efforts suffered from their tardiness. The editing seems to have been done by one assistant, G. W. Eccles, with Bullen's supervision, and it proved to be far more complicated than the mere collection of the title slips would have indicated. Still, it is hard to understand why it should have taken seven years to finish. These had been the crucial years for the much larger project of publishing the general catalogue of printed books in the Museum, and during them Bond and Garnett had been kept on tenterhooks as one catalogue was completed, and the other finally launched.

VII. The Decision to Print, 1879

In August 1878, a new regime began at the British Museum when Edward Bond took over the duties of the principal librarian's office. By the time he had officially been given command at the fall meeting of the trustees in October, Bond had already made a beginning toward his goals, and during the following year he made great advances.

Richard Garnett rejoiced in the change of leadership, for, although Charles Newton had been "strongly in favor of print," and Winter Jones had informed Garnett privately, "shortly before his resignation, that he himself intended to take up the question of introducing printing,"[1] only a new voice could carry the conviction necessary to make the dream a reality. "As keeper of manuscripts, Mr. Bond's attention had never been officially drawn to the catalogue of printed books, but, as a man of letters, he had formed an opinion respecting it; and I am able to state that he came to the Principal Librarianship ... determined to bestow the boon of print upon the catalogue and the public,"[2] said Garnett. Bond had been in the Museum for forty years and had a very fair idea of the working of the Department of

Printed Books. "He had long come to the conclusion that a printed catalogue, and not merely the printing of the additions, was required, and with great tact and administrative skill, he set to work to get his proposals adopted by the Treasury."[3]

George Bullen was not to be so happy with the new regime, for his partiality to the early English catalogue put a barrier between him and Bond, and Bond's efforts to move him toward a different point of view inevitably resulted in friction. This lack of harmony, which became more pronounced as the years went on, was evident in mild form from the start of Bond's tenure. For example, at the end of the records of the Department of Printed Books for 1878 is a paper reading:

> Special Headings in the Catalogue which it is proposed to print, but which Mr. Bullen deems to be at present inexpedient—
> Academies—36 volumes
> Bible—28 volumes
> Liturgies—15 volumes
> Periodical Publications—50 volumes
> Shakspere—2 volumes, but when relaid and rebound will make 4 volumes.

This shows that Bond had already been consulting the officers about the possibilities for printing and that Bullen was being reluctant. Shortly afterward Bond began to put pressure on the keeper, as is shown by a minute of the meeting of the trustees on February 8, 1879, when they

> referred to the Library Sub-Committee a statement, dated the 3rd of February, made by Mr. Bullen, in answer to inquiries by the Principal Librarian, as to the period within which the General Catalogue of

Printed Books would probably be completed, the number of prepared and revised titles now waiting to be incorporated, the number of unsettled queries [i.e. problem entries], etc.[4]

The Society of Arts Again

Outside the Museum as well as inside, library matters were moving forward at this time. In April 1879, the month of Panizzi's death, the Society of Arts at last published the record of its investigations into the feasibililty of a universal catalogue. Its final recommendation was that before going further into the project, "it should be ascertained if the Government would entertain the idea of printing the Catalogue of the Printed Books in the British Museum down to the end of the year 1878, in the cheapest practicable form, suitable for use in all the public libraries at home, in our colonies, and abroad."[5] Appended was a specimen page, probably Cole's, "the numerous typographical and other errors in which," said *Library Journal*, "seem to show that much more editorial labor would be required than appears to be contemplated by the Society of Arts."[6] The *Times* reviewed the report with sarcasm, beginning with the sentence, "The Society of Arts has the provoking but very English quality of never letting drop a subject it has once taken up," and going on to discuss the British Museum catalogue:

If the existing catalogue of the Museum contained every volume a British printing press had ever produced the deluge of current literature would make it obsolete in a dozen years. If there is to be a printed catalogue, the Museum catalogue may as well be copied as it is. To keep up with the times a new edition must soon be issued, and the sparse defects of the distant past can, perhaps, be more conveniently supplied at the same time with the innumerable defects of the near future.[7]

The writer was "melancholy" about the multiplying products of the contemporary press and felt it would be better if everyone stopped reading entirely, although he conceded the necessity of a printed catalogue to advertise what books were in a library.

Garnett's Plan

In the same month, the *New Quarterly Magazine* published Garnett's article called "Public Libraries and their Catalogues," in which he argued in Panizzian fashion: "Every one will admit the intrinsic superiority of a catalogue in print over a catalogue in MS. The question is, whether the advantage may not be bought too dear." He gave statistics of the amount of work involved in publishing the entire catalogue, guessed that the total cost to the nation would be roughly £100,000, and opined that the government would scarcely "incur such an expenditure for such a purpose." Then he stated with deliberate candor that the real need for such an investment of public funds was for the sake of the library itself: "It is desirable, and will shortly become imperative." Noting the reasons for the extravagant amount of space taken up by the manuscript catalogue—the trebled thickness of the leaves when pasted up with slips on both sides, the wide spacing to allow for interpolations, the wastefulness of the transcribers in using up paper, and the existence of countless duplicate entries of full length—Garnett said that the catalogue was "rapidly becoming unmanageable" and would soon outgrow the reading room.[8]

The way he introduced his solution was by noting that although nothing else but print would really alleviate the circumstance, the matter had been confused by referring to the process as "publication," whereas that was not the question at all. What was involved, for the treasury to consider, was the fiscal extravagance of continuing to transcribe when it was obvious that print must eventually be resorted to, which meant paying twice for the same work. The treasury should decide between print and manuscript once and for all. If they decided for print, that could be achieved most easily and cheaply by having all the titles printed before pasting them into the catalogue volumes; then, for the next stage, by printing the manuscript entries from volumes which had reached the point of oversaturation and must be rebound. In this way the bulkiest volumes, ones that could scarcely even be lifted by readers, would be diminished in size first, and over the years the catalogue would gradually become a printed one in the process.

The details of this scheme appear to have been Garnett's own, born of his experience in the reading room, and sharpened by considerable thought on the best way to appeal to those holding the purse strings. He took care to point out that printed accessions lists, if sold by subscription, could help to defray the costs, as would the printing of such special headings as Bible, Shakespeare, Luther, and Homer, which would constitute nearly complete bibliographies and should, therefore, command a respectable sale. These commercial arguments, he tells us in a note added later to the reprint of his article, were emphasized because of "the writer's uncertainty what turn the negotiations with the Treasury for the introduction of printing might take, and his dread of compromising the plans of Sir Edward Bond, who knew nothing of the article until it was in type, when he read it, and returned it without remark."[9] One would think that Bond might have congratulated Garnett for the brilliance of his suggestion, but perhaps he was, indeed, fearful of losing his chance for support through premature publicity. Both Bond and Garnett had, at that time, and with good reason, only a "moderate expectation . . . of any substantial help from the Treasury."[10] Nevertheless, it is clear that Bond had already made up his mind to ask for it and to do as much as he could with whatever he received.

Bond Acts

At the May meeting of the trustees, a reorganization of the reading room service was under discussion, and this gave Bond an opening to make his move toward the printing of the catalogue.

> Mr. Bond begs to call the attention of the Trustees to the increasing difficulty of providing space in the Reading Room for the Manuscript Catalogue of Printed Books.
> There are already 2050 volumes of this catalogue in the room; and it is estimated that there will be 2500 when the incorporation of the new and supplementary catalogue is complete.
> The available space at the catalogue desks is fully occupied; and none of the 450 volumes yet to come can be introduced without displacing something else.
> Each of the 2000 volumes will some day require to be broken up and divided into two. Many volumes in the earlier letters, indeed, are even now nearly ready for this operation and, as the increase of titles is pretty evenly distributed throughout the catalogue, it is quite probable that a large number will be found to require it almost simultaneously. There are also from 200 to 800 volumes of map and music catalogue, to which the same observations apply.
> The growth of these catalogues becomes a great embarrassment; and Mr. Bond would suggest that it

may be advisable to re-consider the possibility of checking it by the use of printing—both for the portions of the General Catalogue already in a sense completed—as the sections of Academies, Bibles, Liturgies and Periodicals and Shakespearean Literature —each of which occupies many volumes—and by substituting printed for written copies of new titles.[11]

The trustees considered this report and "directed the Principal Librarian to submit to the Standing Committee some definite proposal on the subject,"[12] which, of course, he was only too glad to do. And so this modest document of Bond's made bibliographic history.

On July 26, Bond presented to the trustees the report they had requested at the last meeting. He had obtained estimates of the cost of printing the accessions from two firms, and he also presented a memorandum on the cost of revision under the system then in effect. He suggested that he be authorized "to take the necessary steps in order to ascertain whether libraries in the United Kingdom and Abroad, and Publishers, would be willing to subscribe for copies of the titles should the Trustees determine to print them."[13] Authority was granted, and he sent out a circular announcing the project. He invited subscriptions for printed accessions lists of about sixty thousand titles a year, printed on one side of the leaf to admit of being pasted into individual catalogues. To the Committee on a General Catalogue of English Literature of the Library Association, this was a "sign of progress; since it will probably involve, sooner or later, the printing of the Museum's earlier titles."[14] The committee still favored the prior publication of the catalogue of English literature and foresaw an extravagant duplication of effort if both compilations were printed. By now, however, there was no stopping either of them.

When the trustees met again in October, after the

parliamentary recess, Bond told them that the cost for printing sixty thousand titles per year would be £1,250, or £550 more than copying by hand, but that the difference would be made up, he was sure, partly by the saving of time and effort in revision, which a staff report blamed the civil service writers for increasing, and partly by the subscriptions of librarians and booksellers for sets of the printed slips. It was estimated from the nine subscriptions so far received for double sets, and from other indications of interest, that these would amount to about £250 per year.

The trustees gave Bond authority to apply to the treasury for sanction to put £1,200 into the estimates for 1880-81 and to ask for the replacement of seven of the nine copyists by assistants of the second class already on the staff, which would make a net saving in the departmental budget of £1,440. By simple arithmetic Bond had made the adoption of print for accessions and the riddance of the copyists into a strategy for effecting economies.

The response of the treasury came in time for the November meeting of the standing committee. The lords commissioners sanctioned, provisionally, the new allocation for printing entries for the catalogue, "requesting, that when the Museum estimates should be forwarded, that attention might be called to the question whether the new arrangement would effect an immediate saving."[15] Bond was prepared with a memorandum pointing, by more of the same arithmetic, to a saving of £50 immediately, based on yearly salaries and the projected £250 from sales.

By the December meeting Bond had concerted with Bullen the details of the plan for printing. He had secured bids and specimens of printed entries from two firms and had a recommendation from Bullen that the bid of William Clowes and Sons be adopted. This was done. Before being sent to the printer, the entries were to be alphabetized and arranged in seven different classes: Class I, new English books; Class II, new foreign books; Class III, older English books newly acquired; Class IV, older foreign books newly acquired; Class V, main titles from the old catalogue, finally revised; Class VI, finally revised cross-references to main titles in the present catalogue; and Class VII, Oriental language titles. Classes I and II were to be sent in every month, Classes III to VI every three months, never less than 1,250 titles at a time in each of these six classes; and Class VII, "as occasion may require."[16] The printing was to begin in January 1880, at which time the seven copyists were to leave the service of the trustees.

Thus quickly did the whole affair move, once it was presented to the board and the treasury in an efficient and winning manner. Bond's measured remarks, on May 9, about the worsening situation of the catalogue constituted the basis for the inauguration of a printing program less than a year later. These remarks had been preceded, and were reinforced, by Garnett's firm public stand for the urgency of putting the entire catalogue into print for the sake of the Museum itself. The initial requests of a few libraries for advance subscriptions gave Bond an argument that printing might soon be cheaper than transcribing, while the poor performance of the civil service copyists supported his recommendation that their salaries be eliminated from the budget to help pay for the printing.

On the adroitness of these negotiations, Garnett made two telling comments. First, the treasury "could not refuse to entertain" the notion of printing titles of additions to the library, "as it had originally come from itself."[17] Now that at last the trustees had capitulated to the pleas of the treasury to adopt printing in the Museum for immediate economy, the treasury was forced to grant an extra appropriation on the grounds of future savings, something they had theretofore been reluctant to do. Garnett also said of the wisdom of the procedure agreed upon: "The funds on which we relied might at any time fail us, and we might never progress beyond our A. B. C. By making the printing a portion of the daily life of the institution, a piece of administrative routine like cataloguing or binding ,we escape alike ambitious professions and ambitious failures,"[18]

The introduction of printed entries into the British Museum catalogue after so many years of handwritten ones constituted a major change in policy. Merely printing the accessions might not have seemed revolutionary in itself, but it was an irrevocable step forward, which, once taken, opened the way to the publication of the entire catalogue and the maintenance of it in print for the next hundred years.

VIII. Printing Begun, 1880-81

The printing firm of William Clowes and Sons was noted for the quality as well as the speed of its work, and it had long enjoyed the privilege of printing various materials for the government. Its shops boasted electric typesetting machines and twenty steam presses, and could print in such languages as Tongan and Cree, and with hieroglyphics. But best of all, this efficient company had not just printed, but had actually compiled, for the Great Exhibition of 1851, catalogues in English, French, and German—in illustrated and deluxe folio editions—and also guides, plans, and synopses of the exhibits. This experience "made Clowes the recognized authority in that field,"[1] and a natural choice to print the British Museum catalogue. Competition was, of course, required for the bidding, and the other bidder in this case was Eyre and Spottiswoode, printers to Her Majesty's Stationery Office; but Clowes's bid was the lower.

So in January 1880, Clowes began a task that was to occupy a special part of the firm's operation for the next twenty-five years. At the March meeting of the Library Association, "the first portion of the new printed additions to the British Museum Library was shown, and some donations were placed upon the table."[2] The editors of *Library Journal* exclaimed:

> We can imagine how the hearts of the members of the Library Association of the United Kingdom leaped up for joy at the sight of the first sheets of the printed list of accessions to the British Museum, whatever bibliographical criticisms they may, or may not, call forth. This is an earnest of what is to come under the present enterprising management of the Museum, which will make its Library more than it has been before the Capitol of books for all the English-speaking peoples.[3]

Now that the alphabetical catalogue was going into print, however, the librarians lost no time in turning their exhortations toward subject catalogues, saying, with support from the literary press, that the British Museum should now remedy the last fault of its cataloguing system and make plans to publish its general catalogue of books in class arrangement. The obstacles to this goal were insurmountable, and there is still no classed catalogue of the entire library. When George Knottesford Fortescue compiled his series of subject indexes to the modern works added to the library, taken from the printed accessions lists, he did so "for the most part away from the Museum, during non-official hours."[4] It is a great tribute to him that he continued this task until the end of his life, through five five-year volumes and one cumulation covering the years of the publication of the general catalogue, 1881-1900, although he received only a very modest reward from the trustees.

The standing committee met on January 10, 1880, to consider and approve a detailed report which had been drawn up by Bond and Bullen, giving the final version of the scheme for printing the accessions and setting out the division of the tasks involved among the staff. Robert Kennaway Douglas was to superintend the whole process, to insure a constant supply of titles to the printer, and to conduct communications with Clowes. Assistant Keeper G. W. Porter was to keep the cataloguers supplied with books, and Garnett was to "watch over the accuracy of the printed titles."[5] Fortunately, Garnett was soon to assume a greater responsibility for the printing than his original assignment specified.

In the next month the trustees had to decide how many copies of the accessions lists to have printed. Fifty subscriptions had been received and forty copies would be needed for Museum use, so it was agreed:

That provision must be made for not less than 20 additional subscribers for the whole series.
And proposing that, as certain of the 7 sections into which the titles are divided will be in greater demand than others, the number of copies to be printed for

Sections:	I.	II.		be fixed at 200
	III.	IV.	VII.	be fixed at 150
	V.	VI.		be fixed at 100

and that these be offered for purchase separately at subscription prices as under:

I	£2.0.0
II	1.0.0
III-VII each	15.0[6]

The lists of new books, then, that is, sections I and II, were offered at a bargain price of £3 per year. Garnett said eight years later, "For the *original subscribers* the Museum Catalogue is one of the cheapest books in the world."[7] The price had been based on an estimate of a production rate of fifteen parts annually, whereas the rate soon rose to thirty parts, giving a net price of two shillings per part to those who subscribed from the first.

Also in February, a separate decision was made that Bullen should make a special effort to attack the arrears in problem entries: those yet to be revised, cross-references, and "queries." Bullen found that there were 282,636 of these, and surmised that, by taking assistants off other duties, he might be able to complete the revision of the manuscript catalogue "within the next three years or four at the farthest."[8] Such a projection was not likely to please Bond, who demanded still more statistics, this time of the process of incorporating entries and of pasting the slips into the catalogue volumes. He learned that the annual cost of laying down the slips by the binder was £1,781 in addition to the salaries of the four assistants who were engaged in incorporation.

Early in March Bullen reported on the number of "settled queries waiting to be altered in the Catalogue: 29,390," and in the margin of the draft of the report is a note in another hand:

> There were a very great number of these queries when I became Superintendent of the Transcription in 1874. The number has been greatly reduced since, but other such queries have continually arisen during the progress of the work, and are necessarily incidental to it.[9]

This comment had obviously come from the attendant S. J. Aldrich, who in June made four separate reports on the progress of incorporating the printed entries into the manuscript catalogue. By then there were nearly twenty thousand printed title slips ready to be inserted in the catalogue in double columns among the full-width hand written slips. (An illustration of such a page from the music catalogue can be seen in A. Hyatt King, *Printed Music in the*

Printing Begun, 1880-81

British Museum, [London: Clive Bingley, 1979], Plate 7.)
Aldrich was worried about the small margins that had
been left on the printed slips, and said that unless great care
were taken in pasting them down, they would easily be
torn when they had to be removed later for interpolation of
more slips. But Bullen decreed that the incorporation was
to commence on June 21, and assigned five assistants to the
task. The implication in all these reports and remarks is
that Bond had been keenly disappointed in Bullen's
estimate of a three or four years' wait for the end of
Panizzi's transcribed catalogue and had put pressure on
Bullen to diminish the period in any way possible. At the
very least, there must be no more delay in beginning to
incorporate the printed entries into the copies of the
catalogue in the reading room and the cataloguing room.

Stereotyping Considered

Meanwhile, still other ideas were brewing. On June 25,
Assistant Keeper Porter, in the absence of Bullen, made a
report to the trustees on the possibility of stereotyping the
entries for the catalogue. He had conferred with Messrs.
Clowes and had secured from them an estimate of the cost
of making stereotype plates for the first two sections of
printed entries, namely new English and foreign books,
"with a view to their being arranged and issued as a
classified catalogue at a future time."[10] He had been told
that the expense of keeping the type standing for more
than a year would be exorbitant, so he suggested that
about twenty thousand titles be selected for stereotyping,
among them those of recently acquired incunabula and
English books printed before 1640. The advantage of this
plan to the expedition of the early English catalogue is
evident. Just as the assignment of classes to the accession
titles had made it possible for one sorting to serve both the

early English and the general catalogue, the stereotyping scheme appears as another device to satisfy Bullen's needs for his special catalogue.

Although it seems unlikely that Bond supported Porter's idea, he apparently did not oppose it vigorously, for the trustees adopted it at their June meeting, and Bullen subsequently wrote to Clowes communicating this decision and suggesting that one of the partners should call at the Museum to have the selection plan explained in detail.

No more is heard of the stereotyping program until March of 1882, when Bond reminded the trustees of their minute of July 16, 1880, intending the stereotyped titles "for the purpose of publishing a classed catalogue, periodically—and he begs to recommend that stereotyping be in future discontinued, and that the slips of the catalogue of accessions be laid down in a classified form, for use in the reading-room."[11] The latter was never done, and the stereotype casts of entries from those eighteen months were apparently melted down. Richard Claverhouse Jebb, writing as a new trustee in the *Quarterly Review* for October 1898, discussed the advocacy of the stereotype process during the 1850s and then remarked that "this plan was once tried at the British Museum, for the General Catalogue. It was given up because no space for storing the stereotype plates could be found at the printing-office or at the Museum."[12]

The Second Stage

In November 1880, at the time of making up the estimates for the coming year, Bullen submitted to Bond a report which Bond made the basis of his presentation to the trustees, with the suggestion that boys be hired to paste down the entries in the volumes of the catalogue at four pence an hour, in the place of men at eight pence an hour. The Museum's binder, who had charge of the workers in his shop in the building, had consented to the idea and was prepared to substitute three boys for three men at once, with another three at the time for the next incorporation, making six boys and fifteen men on the job. The saving would amount to £275 per year and Bullen, by economies, had already saved £272 during 1880.

This pleasant news for the treasury was prelude to a request for an extension of the printing project. Bond wanted to change the system of dealing with overstuffed catalogue volumes: rather than continuing the cumbersome process of pasting in printed slips among the manuscript ones, which was costing about £900 a year, and dividing the volume when it became unwieldy, he recommended printing the whole of such a volume at once. He thought there might be fifty volumes each year to be treated in this way, and printing them would cost twice as much as intercalating the two kinds of slips, that is, £1800; but before making the proposal, Bond had armed himself with Bullen's plan of hiring boys in the place of men to help meet the excess cost, a device that proved effective. The treasury on November 24 approved the trustees' request to increase the amount set aside in the estimates for printing entries by £1800 "in order to print volumes of the general catalogue as they become filled with titles, reducing the fund for bookbinding, &c . . . by £200, in the Estimates for 1881-1882."[13] Bond was another step closer to his goal of a completely printed catalogue.

By this time Garnett had replaced Douglas as chief editor, in fact, if not in name; for when, on November 10, R. H. Major retired as keeper of maps, and the trustees reduced that department to a subsidiary of Printed Books, in accordance with the wishes of the treasury in 1877, Douglas was put in charge, because his time was "not fully occupied cataloguing Japanese and Chinese [accessions]."[14]

Whatever the sequence of events, Bullen's influence was being circumvented at every opportunity and Garnett's was rising in importance.

No longer, it seems, was Bullen in complete charge of his department's involvement in the printing project. Others were now sending him information that formerly would have originated in his office. In December, for example, a detailed scheme for the new stage of the project was set forth on a sheet at the top of which was written in pencil: "For Mr Bullen." Specifications were given for the size of the projected volumes—the same size as the A-volume of 1841—and for the number of copies, the size of type, the pagination, the running titles, and the paper to be used. A work schedule was made out with the names of the assistants who were to perform the different tasks involved. The tenth item on the list reads: "Copy to be revised by Mr. Garnett, assisted by Dr. Haas, and Mr. Dorset Eccles." The fifteenth reads: "All at present unentered titles to be incorporated."[15]

Further evidence that Bullen was being left out of the planning occurs in a letter which went to the keeper in January of 1881 from Dorset Eccles, one of the most reliable assistants. He wrote:

> As I am not clear about my fresh duties with reference to the preparation of the volumes for printing, may I ask you for some directions thereupon. I did not apply to you for instructions in the first instance, when Mr Garnett brought me a volume of A to begin upon, because I presumed that it was with your sanction that this was done; for I had already been privately told by Mr Douglas (who was concerned at the contemplated interruption to my revision of the Proof Sheets) that, by Mr Bond's direction, I should be called upon to assist this work."[16]

It would appear that Bond was even selecting the assistants

to carry out the new stage of printing, without regard to their current endeavors, for Eccles was to be transferred from the accessions lists to the whole volumes. Even if Douglas remained in charge of the printing of accessions lists, he was being overruled in matters of staffing; for to Bond, the most important activity for the future was the beginning of the volume-by-volume printing, which amounted to the beginning of the publication of the whole catalogue. In this work lay the possibility for the wide dissemination of the catalogue which had been so long desired by the reading public, a role that the accessions lists could by no means fulfill, since the chief interest lay in the older books.

It was lucky for Garnett that there were in the letter *a* enough volumes in dire need of reduction in bulk to make a fair start on the printing of the entire catalogue from *a* to *z* which was to be the third stage of the work under the Bond-Garnett plan. By waiting for a year between demands on the treasury for permission to start new programs, and getting each well under way before suggesting another, the two men were able to carry out the complete enterprise in an amazingly short time, considering the hesitations and postponements that had held it back for decades. The first volume to be prepared entire for the press was "volume 43 of A,"[17] which was to be followed by volume 44.

However, in his anxiety to expedite the printing, Garnett tended toward hasty actions in regard to the staff. He was democratically inclined and had always considered some of the attendants fully as well qualified for some of the cataloguing work as some of the assistants. He now took it upon himself to assign one of the attendants the task of numbering the title slips in alphabetical order for the guidance of the printer. After that he wanted to let the attendant incorporate the printed accession entries into the volumes. If the work was not being done, and a delay in the plan would result, Garnett saw no reason to hesitate in arranging for anyone who was capable, and had the time, to take care of it. Although he may have been given license by Bond to arrange for these tasks to be done by an attendant, the idea more than likely came from Garnett himself.

Dorset Eccles was displeased by this tactic. He wrote to Keeper Bullen that the incorporation had "for over 20 years . . . been done by Assistants, who, moreover, have had to go through a course of special training and instruction before they were deemed . . . qualified to undertake it."[18] Garnett knew that extra help was necessary, but hard to get. He himself was fully occupied as superintendent of the reading room, in addition to his editorial duties, and his burden was very great. Yet in the first year of the extension of the project he managed to supervise the processing of thirty-eight manuscript volumes, which became fourteen printed ones.

Extra Duty Work

Clowes and Son had set up a special department to deal with the British Museum catalogue, and were able to estimate the cost per volume to be printed entire at a little over £12. The firm was required to make a confusing array of copies on two types of paper, some printed on one side for Museum and other library use, some on both sides for general use, and the lot to be delivered at five different places. For example, of sections III and IV, one hundred copies were to be printed on both sides of the paper, one hundred on one side only, and twelve of the latter were to be on thick paper. Copies were to go, in addition to the Museum, to the London Library, the London Institution, and "Mr. Quaritch," the chief bookseller to the Museum, so that he might discover what the library did not have; while twenty-four copies were to be delivered to "G. W. Eccles, Esq." at his home, ten on one side, twelve on both sides, and two on thick paper.[19]

G. W. Eccles, who was also the reviser of the early English catalogue, was the brother of Dorset Eccles, and it may be that both brothers worked on the general catalogue at home, for in April 1881, Bullen asked the trustees to approve funds for the employment of two assistants to prepare copy and revise proofs "in non-official time at their own homes,"[20] quoting three-and-a-half shillings per hour or six pence per printed column as a fair rate of pay. The yearly outlay would come to £250, and the trustees were agreeable to petitioning the treasury for that amount. At the same meeting at which this decision was taken, Bond showed the standing committee a printed volume of letter *b* along with the two handwritten volumes from which it had been derived, as an example of the "diminution in bulk and saving of space effected by the new scheme of printing filled volumes of the Catalogue."[21]

The treasury, under Gladstone as chancellor of the exchequer, acceded to the trustees' request and sanctioned the plan of having the revision and incorporation done by assistants at home "for a period not exceeding four years; and at a cost of not exceeding £250 per annum."[22] But before this the lords commissioners had inquired whether, if this arrangement were likely to be needed for a number of years, "it would not be a preferable course to add an additional second class Assistant to the Establishment."[23] Here the treasury was actually suggesting that the regular staff of the Department of Printed Books be increased, after all the years it had exerted pressure to reduce the number of employees. It could have been Gladstone's farewell gesture to the British Museum, as he resigned his trusteeship on May 6.

Bullen, however, again played the reactionary role: he preferred using his experienced staff in extra hours to starting a new assistant, and, taking a leaf from the treasury books of 1877, he pleaded the economy of paying piecework rates rather than a full salary with annual increments and other benefits. The assistants, he said, could not be spared from their regular duties for work on the printed catalogue during their six hours of attendance at the Museum, but he expected that they would be needed in overtime to a varying extent as the program progressed.

This arrangement continued until 1886, when the Salisbury treasury "declined to continue the grant of £250 per annum for the correction of the proof sheets of the General Printed Catalogue in overtime, that duty having to be performed in the regular official hours."[24] In order to accomplish this, half the time of two assistants would have to be devoted to the proofreading, and since the department was already shorthanded, Bullen was forced to ask for another assistant to keep the work on the catalogue moving, help which he could have had for the preceding five years.

In June of 1881, however, Bullen was able to present to the trustees specimen sheets of his catalogue of early English books, with estimates of the cost of publishing it. "The trustees directed that, 750 copies should be printed, provided Mr. Bullen had sufficient assistance available from other duties to see the work through the press."[25] Bullen replied that he had the necessary help, but that he would like to have an assistant "compile in his own time indexes from the proof sheets." In commenting to the trustees on this request, Bond, whose patience was wearing thin, unveiled Bullen's slight deception:

> The Principal Librarian states that on examination of the title slips prepared for this Catalogue, it is found that the process of condensation and arrangement have been carried no further than to the letter E. . . . Revision to be completed before going to press.[26]

Bond may have cited in support of this decision a minute of

the trustees of February 14, 1863, ordering "that the manuscript of any Catalogue or other work, proposed to be published by order of the Trustees, be completed before printing," for a copy of this resolution was bound into the record book before the committee report. However, if he had reminded the committee of this, he might have been bound to follow the same rule in regard to the main catalogue, which was precisely what he was trying to avoid.

When the time for estimates came around again, Bond and Garnett began to prepare statistics on the progress of the printing program. Garnett worked out the weekly rate of production of complete volumes as one printed volume every three weeks, and at that rate the expenditure by the end of the year would be £1,770 out of the allotted £1,800. "The expenditure and the grant, therefore, would seem to be very accurately adjusted." The two men were hoping, nevertheless, to print more of the special articles in the next financial year and Garnett thought that they should apply for £2,000 "and should be glad of £2,500 if Mr. Bond thinks such an application judicious."[27] Garnett's respect for the tenuousness of the treasury's generosity should have told him that he should be satisfied with the £1,800; and, indeed, either his or Bond's discretion won out, for that was the amount requested and received. The sum nicely covered the capacity of the Department of Printed Books to turn out copy and the capacity of Clowes to set and print all of it on a steady schedule.

IX. INTERIM, 1882-83

A year's experience with the printing of individual volumes had shown Bond that the support he had anticipated from other libraries had not materialized. In January 1882, he had to tell the trustees that at the set price of £8 for the "filled volumes" of the general catalogue and £5 for the accessions lists, the work was going begging. He reported

that the number of subscriptions for the printed portions of the General Catalogue of the Library amounted during the past year to twelve, and of those for the printed Catalogue of Accessions to the Library to twenty-four for forty-nine copies; [and he recommended] that the subscription be reduced for the General Catalogue to £3.10.0, and for the Accessions to £3, with allowance of ten per cent. to agents; single parts to be supplied at 5s/—; and that copies of both series be presented to public libraries in the United Kingdom.

It is proposed to limit the impression of the Accessions Catalogue to 150 copies; and to extend that of the General Catalogue to 250 copies.[1]

This reduction in price had less than the desired effect in stimulating purchases of the work that the library world had been crying for a few years earlier. The reason for the lack of enthusiasm may have been, as much as anything, the sheer quantity of matter involved, for few librarians seem to have had any accurate notion of the true extent of the British Museum catalogue. The accessions sheets also proved awkward to manage, as A. J. Rudolph found at the Newberry Library in Chicago. There more than four hundred sections had accumulated by 1899, each in a separate alphabet, and he was driven to try to cumulate them himself.[2] Furthermore, the individual volumes published had been chosen somewhat at random, and so did not present to other libraries an appealing prospect for purchase.

Bullen Embattled

During 1882 both Garnett and Bullen felt pressure from the policies of modernization going on in the Museum. It must have seemed to them that the principal librarian was intent on reforming the Department of Printed Books. He was becoming testy in his official letters to Bullen conveying the wishes of the trustees which were generally, in those days, his wishes as well; and these requests were becoming more and more unreasonable.

For example, Bond suggested in February that the books in the stacks be rearranged so that those most used would be nearest the reading room, to speed up service to readers. Bullen replied that this would be quite impossible, as there was no available shelving, nor room to build any. He had already commissioned Porter to remove the periodicals from the galleries of the reading room to make way for some of the most frequently used reference books, as Bond had desired. But when this task was still in process, Bond called Bullen in and asked him why a two-year-old decree of the trustees to place in the supplementary reading room in the North Wing "a set of the best books on archaeology and architecture"[3] had not been carried out. Bullen made the mistake of expressing his disapproval of the idea: besides the inconvenience of moving the books, it would involve recataloguing, and the department had cataloguing problems enough without such an added one. Nevertheless, he said, he fully intended to make this difficult adjustment when the completion of other projects allowed time. Bond promptly wrote a letter accusing him of failing the trustees out of purely personal preference.

Almost at the same time Bond chided Bullen for having bound in morocco what he considered little-used books, and got the trustees to urge the keeper to try to reduce the bookbinder's bills for mending and cleaning. On the other hand whereas both Bullen and Garnett were oppressed by the growing accumulation of newspapers, Bond was convinced of their necessity to scholars in conjunction with books, and would not recommend their removal to a separate building. Garnett was anxious to have an appropriation of £50 to pay an assistant to serve as deputy superintendent of the reading room, but the treasury declined to sanction even that small sum for the relief of the overworked superintendent. It seems likely that if Bond had pressed for it, the grant might have been made.

As for the conflict between the general catalogue and the early English catalogue, Garnett, writing in 1899, said that it "continued until 1882, when the decided interference of the Principal Librarian, and the adoption of a suggestion tendered by the present writer, brought the final revision [of the transcribed catalogue] to a speedy completion. . . ."[4] That "suggestion" was to demonstrate the unnecessary slowness of the old manual process and the need on all grounds to speed it up, or else to shift entirely to print.

If Bond's and Garnett's objective of beginning to print the whole general catalogue in alphabetical order were to get under way in the next financial year, something had to be done quickly to finish work on the manuscript catalogue. During most of 1882, while a few A-volumes were being prepared for print on the excuse that they were overstuffed, the two revolutionaries bided their time; but at last they saw no hope of getting ahead without forcing Bullen's hand.

Then began the battle of the principal librarian and the assistant keeper of printed books against the keeper, through the agency of the trustees. Bond asked Bullen for a report on the progress of the old general catalogue, and Bullen duly composed one on October 27 for presentation to the trustees. He found that, at the prevailing rate of progress, it would take three years to finish, although the addition of another reviser might halve the time required.

> Considering the importance of bringing this work to a conclusion Mr Bullen has with great difficulty made an arrangement to have another reviser assigned to the work; namely Mr [A. W. K.] Miller, whose services, however, will be occasionally required in reading the Proofsheets of the Catalogue of Accessions.
>
> On the completion of the Catalogue of early English books, Mr G. Eccles will also be free to assist in the work of the revision.
>
> Considering how near to its completion the final revision now is, Mr Bullen is of opinion, for various reasons, that the printing from A to Z should not be commenced until such revision is fully accomplished.[5]

On November 6, Bond replied that he thought "that efforts ought to be made to commence printing the General Catalogue from its beginning onwards during the coming financial year; and that, if the present staff is insufficient for the undertaking, fresh arrangements should be made."[6]

Bullen, therefore, had to draft another report defending his point of view. He felt that:

Additional Assistants just at present would be of no practical utility as they could not be employed on such a work without great experience.
Mr Bullen has been without the services of an Assistant in the place of Mr Metivier for several months, and now another Assistant, Mr H. Wilson, has resigned. Until these two appointments are filled up, Mr Bullen thinks that it would be inexpedient to ask for an addition to the staff, and thus increase the number of persons who would have to be educated in their duties.[7]

At the bottom of the record of this report in the Department of Printed Books' copy of the minutes of the trustees' meeting is one of Bond's typical memoranda:

Mem. The Principal Librarian submits that in the above report, Mr Bullen seems not to have considered the practicability of employing experienced Assistants of his present staff on the proposed printing of the Catalogue, the new hands being placed on the less difficult work of the Department; and that, as to the second objective, there ought to be no difficulty educating new men in the ordinary duties of an Assistant in the course of a few months, so that the proposed printing might be commenced in the coming financial year. The immense importance of getting the Catalogue into print ought to outweigh considerations of the nature suggested in Mr Bullen's report.

In the margin is the laconic note: "Printing approved. Mr Bullen to report on the means of carrying it out. E. A. Bond, Principal Librarian."
Next we find the draft of a report by Bullen in

November, without day, but finally sent on the twenty-third for a special meeting of the trustees on the twenty-fifth. In it he announced his plan of attack on the new project he had been bidden to carry out. He kept for himself and Assistant R. E. Graves the most responsible tasks, while the music cataloguer, C. J. Evans, would take over Graves's work, retaining general supervision of his former duties as well. Then S. J. Aldrich, the attendant who supervised the incorporation of the printed entries into the transcribed catalogue volumes, would be paid to read proof sheets at home, "in the same manner and at the same rate of remuneration, as that given at present to Messrs Wilson and Dorset Eccles. Mr Graves will read the revises and submit them to the Keeper for approval before marking the same for press." As for finishing the transcription of the last letters of the alphabet, that could be expedited if two new assistants were appointed by the trustees, but it was all going to cost more money:

> Mr Bullen in placing this scheme before the Trustees begs to point out that additional assistance will be required in fetching the books needed for examination in the course of the above work, and he begs to recommend that application should be made to the Treasury for two additional Boy Attendants for the purpose.
>
> Should the means suggested by Mr Bullen be approved by the Trustees a further provision will have to be made in the Estimates for payment of the Assistant to be employed in non-official time in correcting the proof sheets.[8]

This attempt to dissuade the trustees by mentioning every possible added cost to be laid at the door of the new project to print the entire catalogue from the beginning did not succeed; for Bond, being present at the meeting of the standing committee, had the last word. He desired to make a few observations on Bullen's report and, again using figures to strengthen his point, he revealed a conspiracy with Garnett to get around the keeper's objections:

According to this statement three revisers carry on the work at the rate of under forty titles a day.

In order to judge of the difficulties in the way of more speedy progress, Mr Bond, with the assistance of a reviser lately put upon the work, as an auxiliary, tested the system of proceeding in the work of revision, and found that in the space of one hour 103 titles had been examined; of which 55 had been finally disposed of; 35 contained cross-references which were to be verified; and 10 were to be compared with the printed works.

An independent test made in the same manner by Mr Garnett gave a still higher number of titles examined and disposed of, viz. 120.

In view of this evidence of the present unsatisfactory rate of progress of the revising, Mr Bond would recommend that Mr Bullen be desired to report upon the causes of the delay, and upon measures to expedite the work which he considers may be effectual, without resorting to any increase in the staff of his department, or to extra-time allowances.[9]

In the margin is written: "Recommendation approved. Mr Bullen to report accordingly. E. A. Bond, Principal Librarian."

Bullen's reply to the results of these experiments cited some convincing counter-evidence. To demonstrate the "extreme difficulty" of the work, he gave as examples several standard cataloguing problems taken from a brief report by an assistant who noted that in revising the article "United States of America" he had had "to alter more than

600 transcribed titles, and to consult over 200 books; a work occupying more than 3 weeks."[10]

Garnett had drawn into the fray the assistant Arthur W. K. Miller, who was to follow Garnett and Fortescue in the keepership of printed books and Garnett as editor of the printed catalogue, and who was already attempting to reduce the arrears in revision. Miller had helped Bond in his personal investigation into the process of preparing the entries for the catalogue, and Bullen, in retaliation, elicited from Miller a statement "that the titles put aside during the Principal Librarian's test, would occupy many hours of further examination, and would represent at least one whole day's work."[11]

So Bond and Garnett were caught out: their test had been rigged. Bullen's contention that the test performance could not "be taken as a safe basis for estimating the rate of progress which it is possible to achieve in the final revision" swayed the trustees, who accepted his subsequent proposals:

> Mr Bullen begs to assure the Trustees that he is fully as anxious as the Principal Librarian to bring the work of final revision to a conclusion. In a former report he mentioned that he had assigned Mr Miller to this work, and he now finds that he is also able to employ Mr Gregory Eccles during a portion of his time upon the final revision.
>
> He also proposes to relieve the Final Revisers from a laborious part of the work now pressing upon them by employing a Junior Assistant in comparing the cross-references with the main-titles in the various parts of the Catalogue.
>
> By these means Mr Bullen trusts that the work of final revision may be accelerated.[12]

A note in the margin reads: "Mr Bullen to report as to

success of measures proposed by him for expediting the printing of the Catalogue. E. A. Bond, Principal Librarian." The whole Bond-Garnett exercise had a strong Panizzian flair; it was a tour de force executed at the last possible minute so that funds for the printing from *a* to *z* might be included in the new year's budget, and it was almost successful. Garnett deserves credit for his ingenuity in devising the test, but it also suited Bond's statistical style of argument. If its object had been merely to force Bullen into assigning competent personnel to finish up the transcribed catalogue, that had been achieved. Although Bullen had won a delay in the inception of the third stage of the printing, he had been clearly warned that Bond would tolerate a wait of one year at the most, not of three years.

Garnett often praised "the peculiarly quiet manner" in which Bond effected changes at the British Museum: "A question which had been so long and clamorously agitated while unripe was, being ripe, settled in a few conversations, and with a little official correspondence, so noiselessly and unostentatiously, that many of those most interested in the matter have never heard of it."[13] The adverb "relentlessly" might well have been added to the description of Bond's manner, for while Bullen was never subjected to the kind of publicity that tended to surround anyone who stood in Antonio Panizzi's way, he surely felt from Bond the same "steam-roller" tactics that had been ascribed to the great Italian. Bond was a man who contrived to get what he wanted by prodding his subordinates while ingratiating himself with the trustees, and his ability to succeed was as remarkable as his tenacity of purpose.

Progress at Last

The junior assistant was so efficient in verifying cross-references that Bullen was able, by February 1883, to report that "the number of entries made available for printing in a given time has increased by about a third." Letter *x* was in print, letters *v* and *w* were almost finished, and the comparatively brief *y* would be undertaken by Miller, whose assignment full-time as reviser had "much accelerated" the work. The trustees appreciated Bullen's efforts and achievement, but could not resist another exhortation:

> Resolved, that the Trustees learn with satisfaction that the measures taken for expediting revision have been successful; and desire to impress on the Keeper of the Department the importance of giving constant attention to methods for simplifying the work of his staff.[14]

The good results of Bullen's suggestions had been aided by a grant increased from the original £1,800 for printing accessions to £3,700, and of this amount £300 was left at the end of the year, from economies and diminished purchases. Bullen proposed spending the balance to print twenty-five thousand accumulated music titles. By now the efficiency of Clowes had rendered the cost of printing lower than that of transcribing, but the music catalogue was still in manuscript, its 372 volumes occupying an undue amount of space in the reading room. "Mr Bullen is of opinion that the time has now arrived when such a work may be properly commenced,"[15] Garnett having provided him with an educated guess that it would require eight years at £500 a year. The proposal was accepted and printing of both the music and the map accessions was begun in 1884. The two-volume map catalogue by Douglas was issued in the following year.

The printing of the general catalogue of printed books in alphabetical order had not yet gotten under way, however. Garnett's annual report for 1883 made a point of the fact that reading the proofs of the early English catalogue had interfered with the preparation of the general catalogue, but stated that he had superintended, "under Mr Bullen's direction," the printing of the larger work. Therefore, he was by then officially in charge of the project.

When the time came to make up the estimates for 1884-85, Bullen recommended that the current grant for printing be continued. Two months later he wrote to Bond, probably at his request, that an extra £800 would be advisable.

> My reasons for recommending the increase are that next year I shall have at my disposal the services of three or four of the most experienced Assistants in the Library at present engaged in the final revision and incorporation of the Old Catalogue titles and in the Early English Catalogue. Both these works are rapidly approaching completion and I propose then to devote as much labour in the Department as possible towards the progress of printing the General Catalogue of the Library. With the additional aid referred to I do not doubt that I shall be able to proceed much more rapidly than at present if the Government will consent to the necessary increase for printing. The Trustees and the Government have so fully recognized the importance of this great work that I trust you will concur with me in submitting the amended estimate to the favourable consideration of the Trustees.[16]

The sarcasm of the last sentence could not have escaped Bond or the members of the board, and the fact that the letter was written almost at the end of the year indicates that it was inspired by the principal librarian himself out of frustration at Bullen's insistence on finishing the manuscript catalogue before embarking on another stage of the printing program. And in the coming year Bond was to have his way.

X. THE THIRD STAGE, 1884-85

The treasury was not so generous as Bullen and Bond had hoped, but in the light of his favorable financial position, Chancellor Hugh Childers allowed the grant to be raised to £4,000, and in January 1884 the printing of the entire general catalogue from *a* to *z* was finally begun. During the year thirty volumes, rather than the fifteen of previous years, were produced, and this lowered the cost from £110 per volume to £90. The *Times* attributed this success to "the great care and attention which Messrs. Clowes, the printers, have bestowed upon the work," and equally to "the exertions of Mr Garnett."[1] Such praise must have been very gratifying to the largely unrewarded editor.

Also during 1884 the last volume of the early English catalogue came off the press and copies of the three-volume set were presented by the trustees to Bullen; to the two assistant keepers, Porter and Douglas; to G. W. Eccles, who had been its chief compiler; to Henry Stevens, the American book dealer in London, from whom a large number of rare books had recently been purchased; to Edward Arber, editor of the *Stationers' Registers*; and to "Dr. Ginsberg," probably the Biblical scholar, Christian David

Ginsburg, who had recently saved the Museum from the embarrassment of purchasing some faked Old Testament fragments. A month after this lot of donations was made, a set was given, at Bullen's suggestion, to J. O. Halliwell-Phillipps, who was working on the last edition of his *Outlines of the Life of Shakespeare*. In 1895 the Bibliographical Society asked for and received six copies of the catalogue to help in their compilation of handlists of books printed in England from 1500 to 1556, the period before that covered by Arber's great work.

In November the trustees acceded to Bond's belated request that Garnett "be relieved from the Superintendency of the Reading Room on the grounds of his being occupied with other duties connected with the progress of the Printed Catalogue, the selection of foreign books, and the general business of the Department." This meant that at last Garnett was to receive recognition for his editorial work, although the amount of overt praise bestowed on him for this was far less than it should have been. At least he was honored by the presence of his superiors, Bond and Bullen, at a small ceremony in recognition of his obliging service to the patrons of the reading room, who had taken up a collection to pay for a testimonial of their appreciation. Yet Bond, who seemingly lost no opportunity to criticize the conduct of the Department of Printed Books to the trustees, commented on the assistant chosen to succeed Garnett as superintendent, G. K. Fortescue, that his work as placer had qualified him "to assist Readers in their researches—as well as to detect causes of delay in supplying Readers' orders for books."[2]

Staffing Problems

Meanwhile the unfortunate Bullen had been plagued by more shortages of staff and the treasury was becoming parsimonious again, as Childers attempted to balance the budget and pressures built up toward the fall of the Gladstone government. The new White Wing of the Museum building was about to be opened, with a newspaper reading room which required that an assistant and three attendants be assigned to superintend the service there; but whereas the appointment of the attendants was approved, that of the assistant was deferred by the trustees. Furthermore, masses of books were being sent by the government in India under the copyright law, but the treasury had refused to grant any extra money for cataloguing them. The department had not only lost the chief incorporator on the manuscript catalogue in August, but the Scandinavian specialist as well, the only good result of the latter misfortune being that Gregory Eccles, who had done the major work on the early English catalogue and some of the most demanding and complex work on the general catalogue, was, after twenty-seven years' service, given a promotion to the vacant higher post.

At the November meeting of the standing committee there was presented for discussion another unpleasant treasury letter asking for reconsideration of the employ-ment of the assistants in overtime on revising the catalogue, and a full report "as to the present state and probable duration of the work, and suggesting payment by the piece rather than by the hour." To this Bullen replied, "the staff of the Department is fully occupied; and the suppression of overtime for revising would seriously hinder the progress of printing."[3]

The treasury answered that they would postpone providing for the extension of the overtime until they had received the trustees' opinion on a proposal "to re-transfer Mr Gosse to the Museum with specific reference to this duty."[4] This proposal had been made in September and considered by the trustees in October, apparently without notifying Bullen. Edmund Gosse had been a transcriber at the British Museum from 1867 to 1875, and had been one of the disaffected young men who had caused embarrassment to the department at the time of the Poles incident. He had moved to the Board of Trade as a translator and, his talents no longer being needed there, it seemed reasonable to the treasury that he should go back to the Museum. The trustees were willing enough "to take him as a supplementary officer," but not to give him a position which could be filled by someone already on the staff. Bullen, however, took grave exception to the proposition, saying:

> That the work of revision can only be done by experienced Assistants who have had long and intimate acquaintance with the details of the Catalogue.
>
> That the present arrangement was adopted in preference to the Treasury suggestion of adding an Assistant to the permanent staff.
>
> That Mr Gosse, when in the Trustees' service, was occupied with transcribing titles, an elementary work now superseded by printing, and that reasons against employing a new Assistant as a reviser would apply almost equally to Mr Gosse.
>
> That at the present time, when the printing is being accelerated, any interference with the modus operandi would be disastrous.[5]

Though no disparagement was meant, said Bullen, "Mr Gosse's transfer to the British Museum will not meet the present peculiar needs of the Museum Service in relation to the printing of the General Catalogue."

The strength of Bullen's objections, in contrast to his usually decorous expression, indicates a certain degree of pique; and it was effective, for Gosse did not return to the Museum. In Gosse's behalf, it should be said that he would probably not have consented to return to a kind of work that he hated. He was considering a change of employment because his literary work caused friction with his superiors, who were doubtless behind the treasury letter. At the time of this discussion, Gosse was lecturing in the United States to enthusiastic audiences. He remained at the Board of Trade until 1887, having managed, as he wrote, "to make myself invisible"[6] while the impetus to move him diminished.

In order to hasten the progress of the catalogue, Bullen was asking for still another £1,000 for 1885-86, so he had to justify his staff arrangements; and in December he was requested to "draw out for the Treasury a scheme showing the actual employment of your staff of Assistants,"[7] which he did. The grant was not increased, but a temporary assistant for the White Wing reading room was approved on December 27, as was the appropriation for the overtime of the regular assistants on the printed catalogue. The latter was, however, limited to one year, with the expressed hope that this custom would be dispensed with after that time. Bullen pointed out that remuneration for this work was by the amount of copy turned out—sixpence per column—and therefore reflected real accomplishment. He also remarked that "the recent transfer of Mr Garnett from the Reading Room to the Library will enable that gentleman to devote much more time to the superintendence of the printing."[8] Unfortunately, Garnett's released time was not enough to speed the process measurably and Bullen still felt the need of the overtime grant for 1886. Bond, facing a meeting of the standing committee in October 1885 with a new Conservative government in power, declined to support the grant on that occasion, telling Bullen that the end of the amalgamation of the old and new catalogues and the completion of the catalogue of early English books should afford enough relief to make the entire project possible during regular hours.

Garnett's Report

Actually, the printing grant had reached its most effective level. Garnett said in September 1885 that "last year it required the greatest exertions"[9] to use it up. This remark was made in a report on the progress of the catalogue to the American Library Association at their Lake George Conference. He explained that when printing began there was enough handwritten matter to fill 9,000 sheets or 144,000 columns at twenty-one entries to the column. But the catalogue was a progressive one: it "gathers up subsequent accessions within its sphere as it proceeds"—about forty thousand new titles per year. Therefore the true extent of the catalogue could not be judged at any one moment, but depended on the rate of printing, for the new titles had to be printed twice—as accessions and then, in place, as part of the alphabetical catalogue volumes.

The thirty volumes published during 1884 contained about one hundred and fifty thousand entries. Garnett's hope was to finish by the end of the century, though this might require, he thought, additional funds and staff to accomplish. It was "no trifling undertaking," revising the entries written over a span of forty years by as many hands. Some of them took "research requiring much time, and generally the more in proportion to the insignificance of the matter to which they relate. . . . The greatest difficulty, however, has not been literary or bibliographical revision, but the arrangement of the articles," for the system used for the manuscript catalogue had had to be changed in several ways. Garnett gave credit to the assistants who had prepared the special headings, but spoke modestly of his own contribution, which was obviously large and crucial. It consisted, in fact, of the combined assignments originally given to himself and to Douglas in 1880:

> My business has been . . . to provide for the regular delivery of copy to the printer, and the speedy return of proofs and revises, and to bestow such literary revision as I am able upon the whole; partially and imperfectly before it goes to press, more fully and deliberately when it appears in the shape of a revise. It is very rarely that more than one revise has been asked for. One principle has always governed my work: to prefer rapidity and regularity to minute accuracy, and to take the risk of error rather than encounter the certainty of accumulation and arrear in the contingency of the subscriber receiving less for his annual subscription than we desire to give him.

Admitting that stricter revision would have been desirable, he pleaded in extenuation that "this is neither a catalogue by nor for specialists," and indeed its value lay in its mere existence in print in a creditable, if far from perfect, form. Behind all the rush, of course, but impossible to mention publicly, was the desire of the principal librarian to get the job finished. But no amount of money or overtime by assistants could have made up for the willingness and devotion, the energy and expertise, that Richard Garnett gave to the project.

After the bulkiest volumes had been printed, he said, the letter *a* was begun, and at the same time, "Virgil to Z," for although the revision of the transcribed entries had been completed at the end of 1883, the amalgamation of them with the rest of the catalogue had only reached mid-*v*, so some double printing was avoided by putting the rest of the letter directly into print. This made the strange result that, in the alphabetical printing of the catalogue, "the end . . . was published before the beginning." The headings "Academies" and "Bible" had been set aside, but "Academies" was almost done and Assistant Russell Martineau had undertaken the vast heading "Bible," which was not completed, in three parts and appendix, until 1899. By mid-1885, 295 manuscript volumes had been printed into 78, averaging five thousand entries each, which meant that by the end of that year about one-seventh of the whole would be done. The *Times* had earlier reported that of the 247 copies so far printed, half had been given free to libraries in the United Kingdom, and only 75 had been sold to the public by subscription.[10]

An unforeseen problem then loomed, according to Garnett. The expected small number of subscribers was slowly increasing and those who had started late would have to purchase the back volumes at a higher cost than that which had been set at the beginning. It would, therefore, cost £20 instead of £3 to start a subscription including all the issued volumes, and as time went on this difficulty would make it impossible for any but very wealthy libraries to subscribe. Furthermore, the first year's limited output of fifteen copies of each part would soon be out of print. Garnett's idea to help that situation, one that Bond would surely have supported, was the creation of a department of photography at the Museum to duplicate such works. Even the special articles were rapidly being sold out, said Garnett, "Bacon," "Byron," "Swedenborg," and "Xenophon" being already in that category. In conclusion he opined that a new edition of the entire catalogue should be issued every twenty-five years, the ideal which had been cherished from the start at the Museum, but had never been, and was not to be, achieved.

XI. WINDING UP

All in all, the printing project was proceeding more successfully than might have been expected, given all the vicissitudes attendant upon it. As it turned out, however, the two men most directly responsible for its inauguration and its success were not to be in office when the final day came. Bond retired in 1888, leaving his position and the completion of the great catalogue in the hands of the next principal librarian, his former colleague in the Department of Manuscripts, Edward Maunde Thompson. Bullen then felt free to make a change in the system of dividing the accessions into sections by kind of publication. Waiting for enough entries to accumulate to make a batch of 1,250 in each section was causing unnecessary delay in the incorporation of new titles into the catalogue. If the sections were all thrown together, reasoned Bullen, a batch could be constituted much more quickly, "enough for a Part every fortnight,"[1] and this would allow the maintenance of an exact schedule for sending, returning, and resending to the printer revised copy. The system was instituted and worked exceptionally well.

Two years later Bullen retired and Richard Garnett at

last became keeper of printed books. By this time he was looking forward longingly to the end of the printing of "GK 1," even though he had given over the editorship to Arthur Miller. In a third-person report to the trustees in 1891 he confessed that

> the effect of undertaking the printing of the catalogue and of the regular incorporation of titles—invaluable improvements as they are—has been to deprive his department of the elasticity which it formerly possessed. A certain number of assistants must be kept employed on work which can on no account be intermitted, and the ability to meet exigencies in other branches of departmental work is proportionately decreased. . . . Mr Garnett fears that unless a remedy be promptly applied, the arrears of work which he found existing on his appointment will be bequeathed with large additions to his successor.[2]

Despite the able endeavors of Miller as editor and G. F. Barwick as chief reviser, the progressive publication program which Garnett had so enthusiastically furthered in the seventies had begun to lose its glamor as its demands continually constrained the department. The funds it required could well have been used to support other necessary activities, but they were not so much regretted as was its absorption of the best energies of the library for twenty long years. That the printed catalogue was given priority during this period for the benefit, not just of the Museum itself, as Garnett had argued in 1879, but of readers everywhere and for all time, is a tribute to the admirable concept of service that characterizes the Department of Printed Books.

Early in 1895 three assistants were lost to the department in quick succession, reducing the total number of staff, which had been forty in 1886, to an insupportable low of thirty-four. Six of these were committed to the printed catalogue, and Garnett, in desperation, requested extraordinary help: either an early meeting of the trustees or an early examination by the civil service commissioners to build up the staff again. Yet the treasury instead wanted Garnett to manage with still fewer assistants. In order to "show the Treasury our good faith," Garnett was willing to admit that in about three years, when the catalogue was entirely ready for the press, he might be able to manage without three of the six men who were employed on it, although "it must not for a moment be supposed that all these gentlemen could be dispensed with,"[3] as much would remain to be done.

In the fall of the year, Garnett was asked for a report on the advantages of reprinting either the accessions lists or the whole catalogue. He wrote:

To reprint the accessions in a separate form would be of no advantage to the Museum, as the titles would remain in the working copies of the General Catalogue exactly as they are now, and the appendix would seldom be consulted for any purpose. As regards the public, it would be a great advantage to those libraries which already possess the General Catalogue, but it is doubtful whether many of these would purchase it. From its imperfect and heterogeneous character it would be of hardly any use to any one outside these libraries, and the sale would probably be exceedingly small. I cannot think, therefore, that such a publication would bring any considerable advantage to the public, or any credit to the Museum.

The reprinting of the entire catalogue would also be unattended by any advantage to the service of the Museum, except the diminution of the cost of removing accession titles. But it would be a great and magnificent undertaking, which would confer great advantages upon literature and great honour upon the trustees.[4]

In conclusion Garnett referred to the eternal problem of cost by suggesting that "the expense might be diminished by recent improvements in printing machinery, such as the linotype." Although this did not occur during his lifetime, fifty years later new printing technology became the most important factor in the economics of republication of the British Museum catalogue.

By 1896 the White Wing was filling up rapidly, and Garnett had to find a way to dispose of the three bound copies of the old manuscript catalogue, which he described for the principal librarian:

No. 1, bound in purple formerly stood in the Reading Room. [This was more commonly known as the "blue copy."]

No. 2, bound in red, in the Catalogue room of the Old Library.

No. 3, bound in green, in the 'Title Room' on the basement of the New Library.

The 'Fourth Copy' consists of the transcribed or printed slips, each separately mounted and arranged in boxes according to the order in which the books stand on the shelves. These slips which form a subject index of the whole library are used for such alterations of press marks as are found necessary.

Of the three bound copies No. 1 has been used as 'copy' for the printers and the sheets have been destroyed from time to time; portions of No. 2 have been used and destroyed in the same way, so that No. 3 alone remains intact. Storage room for this, together with the greater part of Catalogue No. 2, has hitherto been found in the basement of the Newspaper Room in the White Wing but it is now necessary to remove both copies to make room for the London Newspapers of 1895 and 1896.

I think it would be desirable to preserve one bound copy of the old Catalogue for which room can be found in two hitherto unused cupboards, one between the first and second Supplementary Rooms, the other on the Basement beneath the Large Room. I would therefore suggest that Copy No. 3 be removed to these cupboards and that the other copy, No.2, including the covers of the volumes for which I can find no useful purpose, should be destroyed.[5]

"Copy No. 3" remained in the cupboards until 1911, when, on April 8, the anniversary of Panizzi's death, the trustees ordered that it, too, be destroyed, to free the space for other uses. Such was the ignominious end of the famous "New General Catalogue of Printed Books" in its original form. It was succeeded by three sets of volumes of printed entries, the green one to be "authoritative"[6] and to be used as copy for the second edition of the published catalogue.

The year 1897 brought the decision to reprint the accessions lists issued in 1881, which had long been out of print. This time they were to be produced in lots of one hundred copies each in order to raise the stock to equal that of the rest of the parts.

On New Year's Day, 1898, Queen Victoria belatedly conferred on Edward Bond the order of Knight Commander of the Bath. The next day he died peacefully at his house in the assurance that the catalogue would be completed and that his efforts on behalf of the nation were appreciated. In that same year the title "Principal Librarian and Secretary [to the trustees]" was changed to "Director and Principal Librarian," and a general salary increase was given to the officers of the British Museum, indicating that the marquis of Salisbury's second ministry was more tolerant of such thorough financial reform in a single institution than governments of the seventies had been. Even the cause of world bibliography seemed to be advancing: Richard Garnett took note of the publication of a part of the catalogue of the Bibliothèque Nationale in Paris, and remarked with pride that the event merely indicated "how far even that great library is behind that of the Museum in the extent and variety of the information which it offers to students."[7]

During the nineties the trustees had decided to donate some more copies of the catalogue. The Office Internationale de Bibliographie in Brussels was given "a set of excerpts from the printed Catalogue . . . with the two Volumes of the Subject Indexes,"[8] and the next year requested to be allowed to purchase two more copies. Four libraries in Australia purchased sets and three sets were donated there. Two copies were donated to Canada, and one each to New Zealand and India. When the end of the publication program was in clear view, in mid-1900, Maunde Thompson got permission to offer sets of the catalogue to certain of the colonies that had not yet received them. With sixty copies left in stock, it seemed desirable to spread the largesse of the trustees to at least ten more colonial institutions. The secretary of state for the colonies was asked to help in the selection of the list, and the final decision was to send fourteen sets, four of them to South Africa, three to Canada, three to the West Indies, two to India, and one each to Ceylon and Tasmania.

Up to 1900, eighty-five copies had been presented and seventy-nine subscribed for. Then, with the printing of the main catalogue almost completed, Clowes began to print the accessions since 1881 in the form of a supplement. Parts 1 and 2 were ready by March of 1900 and Thompson suggested that they, and afterward the rest of the supplement, be presented to those libraries which had received copies of the main catalogue. Thus the generosity of the British government continued: it had expended large sums on a catalogue of the Museum library, and then had given away more copies than had been purchased. The estimates for 1901-2, drawn up in September 1900, included only £1,000 for printing entries and £1,250 for the supplement, although they also contained £750 for publishing Fortescue's cumulated subject index for 1881-1900. The headings "England" and "Liturgies" were at last in print, and when the index to the periodical publications was completed in December of 1900, said Fortescue, who was now keeper of printed books, "the whole of the General Catalogue will then be in type."[9] By that time some of the printed volumes in the reading room catalogue had become overcrowded again and needed to be reprinted, and keeping up with these would cost another £300 per year. So the old tale was repeated in the new century.

XII. EPILOGUE

March 20, 1899, was Richard Garnett's last day in the Department of Printed Books at the British Museum. His wife's serious illness made him decide to retire before the mandatory time and before the publication project was finished. Although its completion was assured, his hopes for the future of the catalogue were not destined to be carried out, for he was always convinced of the necessity of a subject index to accompany the author catalogue, and he believed that both the general catalogue and the early English catalogue should be reprinted within a few years of the end of main publishing program.

There is but one way of obtaining a perfect index to the condition of the national library at a given time: the catalogue must be reprinted along with the numerous accessions which have been accumulating while the first edition has been going through the press—a national undertaking which will commend itself to men of letters more readily than to ministers of finance. Should, however, the completion of the catalogue nearly coincide with the commencement of the twentieth century, it may be hoped that this will be one of the many ways in which, if the new century does not, like its predecessors, find the nation traversing a crisis, the epoch will assuredly be commemorated. It would remain to provide for the regular reprinting of the catalogue with its accessions at intervals, say of a quarter of a century. England would then possess a complete index to the growth of the national library, and the world would have the nearest approach to a register of all literature that, in the absence of any feasible scheme for a universal catalogue by co-operation among public libraries, it seems likely to obtain.[1]

Garnett could speak idealistically of a perpetual catalogue which others to come after him would have to produce, but his successors were not able to sustain the momentum that he and Bond had initiated. The library needed a period of rest from the great endeavor before starting on another edition.

The completion of "GK 1," the *British Museum: General Catalogue of Printed Books,* in December of 1900 occasioned no such celebration as Garnett had anticipated. Its "truly millenial aspect"[2] had been lost in the long bit-by-bit process of production necessitated by the vast bulk of the library. The 374 volumes of the complete edition contained between two and four million entries;[3] they sold for £84, or £71 to subscribers, and had cost the British nation around £50,000, or half what had been projected at the beginning. One user commented that the catalogue "is printed in large, clear type, double columns, well spaced, and its open page is a comfort to the eye,"[4] quite different from the format first proposed by the Society of Arts. There is no doubt that it was quietly appreciated. By 1909 it was out of print. The supplement covering additions to the library from 1882 to 1899 was completed in 1905 in ten volumes, and sold by subscription at £10.

By the second decade of the twentieth century there were so many more libraries wanting copies of the British Museum catalogue that the trustees decided to publish a new edition, for exactly the opposite reason from Garnett's in 1879:

> not so much to satisfy the internal requirements of the Museum, as in response to a demand, from all quarters of the globe, for a bibliographical tool, already in their possession, which other great libraries find to be indispensable.
>
> To meet this demand satisfactorily it must be their aim to produce a catalogue, more than half as large again as its predecessor, embodying essential improvements and adequately consistent in method, within a reasonable limit of time.
>
> The striking of this balance must always be the chief problem in such an undertaking. But "the Catalogue of an institution like the British Museum, dealing with a mass of matter already accumulated, and intended to register an ever-accumulating mass of matter for ever and ever, must not aspire at perfection, and can never attain finality"; and a new edition of the Catalogue being asked for, these words of Richard Garnett are sufficient justification of this attempt to provide it.[5]

Thus the situation in 1931, when the printing of the second edition began, was quite different to that of 1881: the trustees and the treasury could now see the value in publishing a work of reference for the world, and were willing to spend the nation's resources for such an end. The scholarly cataloguers, however, were overly concerned with revision of Garnett's hasty editing, and they produced barely three volumes a year. So when the great war of 1939-45 interrupted their work, "GK 2" had reached only as far as the letter *c*, and afterward the editing progressed so slowly that by 1954 the only sensible recourse seemed to be to photolithography.

The third edition, "GK 3," was begun in 1957 by photographing the entries of the working catalogue, which had been arranged in perfect alphabetical sequence by mechanical means developed by Messrs. Balding and Mansell, the new printers of library catalogues in Great Britain. This method of duplication was so rapid that it produced four volumes a month of five hundred pages each. The edition began with volume 52, where "GK 2" had left off, but the first fifty-one volumes were reprinted at the end of the publication sequence. Sir Frank Francis said of the new edition:

> The method of production—the reproduction photo-lithographically of printed matter produced on paper of varying colour and quality over a period of seventy years and with many alterations in manuscript—makes no pretensions to 'fine' printing. Its virtue lies in its completeness and the fact that it will have been produced in so short a time. It puts in the hands of users in every quarter of the globe the complete and up-to-date catalogue of the British Museum as it was in daily use in the Reading Room up to the end of 1955. Supplements both annual and cumulative are planned, thus enabling subscribers to have the complete catalogue at their disposal at any time.[6]

This edition was published between 1961 and 1967 and from it, in 1968, was derived a "compact" edition. Previously, in 1946, Edwards Brothers of Ann Arbor, Michigan, had found it profitable to reproduce by photo-lithography, in reduced format, the original edition of the printed catalogue, "GK 1."

Today what might be called "GK 4" is under way, although that nickname has been abandoned in favor of

Epilogue

"BLC," the *British Library General Catalogue of Printed Books to 1975*, combining "GK 3" and its three supplements, revised and corrected, with entries for books acquired up to 1970 and most of those that were added from 1971 to 1975. The prepublication price for subscribers in the Americas was $55.00 per volume, or just under $20,000.00 for the set. The first of 360 volumes came from the press under the imprint of K. G. Saur and Clive Bingley in 1979, in the same format as that of "GK 3," and at a projected rate of six or seven volumes per month.

Meanwhile, the reading room catalogue has grown once more to two thousand volumes, a number that Richard Garnett thought would take three centuries to accumulate. But the officers of the Department of Printed Books are in no fear that it will run the readers out of the room. Their hope is that by the end of the twentieth century a new building for the British Library, Reference Division, will relieve the present crowding of readers, books, and catalogue alike.

Chronology

1753	British Museum incorporated.
1787	First printed catalogue of the library, 2 vols. "Ayscough."
1813-19	Second catalogue of the library, 7 vols. Ellis and Baber.
1831	Panizzi enters Department of Printed Books.
1834	Trustees decree a new catalogue.
1835-36	Select Committee of the House of Commons on the British Museum.
1837	Panizzi made keeper of printed books.
1838	Trustees demand a printed catalogue. Rye, Bullen, and the elder Garnett enter the Department of Printed Books.
1839	Trustees decree publication of the catalogue in alphabetical order of the entries, not the books. "91 Rules" adopted.
1841	First volume of new catalogue published; Panizzi stops the printing.

1847-49	Royal Commission on the British Museum.
1850	Report of the commission published; Dilke reviews it in the *Athenaeum*. Jones made assistant keeper, Bond "Egerton Librarian"; Garnett, Sr., dies.
1851	Garnett the younger enters the Department of Printed Books.
1852	Society of Arts hears Sir Henry Cole on universal catalogue. Disraeli is chancellor of the exchequer, February to December. Gladstone becomes a Peelite; at Board of Trade till December, then chancellor of the exchequer. Lowe to House of Commons; to Board of Trade after Gladstone.
1853	Northcote-Trevelyan Report.
1854	Bond made assistant keeper of manuscripts. Crimean War begins.
1855	Order in Council establishes Civil Service examinations. Northcote enters Parliament. Gladstone's second term as chancellor of the exchequer, January-February.
1856	Panizzi is made principal librarian, Jones appointed keeper of printed books. Gladstone becomes a trustee of the British Museum.
1857	New reading room opened; Museum employees put under civil service.
1858	Garnett's first volume of lyrics published. Disraeli's second term as chancellor of the exchequer.
1859	Gladstone becomes a Liberal; is chancellor of the exchequer under Palmerston.

Northcote is financial secretary to the treasury, Lowe vice-president of the Committee for Education.

1861   Cambridge University Library begins printing accessions.

Museum assistants, first class, divided into upper and lower sections.

Maunde Thompson enters Department of Manuscripts.

Gladstone inspects Natural History Department with Owen.

1863   Disraeli becomes a trustee of the British Museum.

1865   Palmerston dies; Gladstone leader of the House of Commons as well as chancellor of the exchequer.

Lord John Russell is prime minister.

Childers financial secretary to the treasury.

1866   Panizzi retires; Jones becomes principal librarian.

Madden retires; Bond becomes keeper of manuscripts.

Rye is made assistant keeper and superintendent of reading room.

In July, Disraeli becomes chancellor of the exchequer under Derby; purchases Blacas collection.

1868   Classed catalogue begun in the Department of Manuscripts.

Disraeli prime minister February to December, then Gladstone.

Lowe made chancellor of the exchequer in Liberal cabinet.

W. H. Smith to Parliament.

1869   Rye becomes keeper of printed books.

Lingen made permanent secretary to the treasury.

1870	Porter made assistant keeper; Fortescue joins the department.
	Assistants in Manuscripts compiling indexes out of regular hours.
	Order in Council decrees open examinations for civil service appointments.
1871	Roy made assistant keeper of printed books in preference to Garnett.
	Order in Council regarding civil service writers.
1872	
April 8	Treasury requests report on cost of Museum copying.
April	Bradshaw's memorial to trustees regarding incunabula.
May 25	Meeting of Temporary Clerks and Civil Service Writers' Association.
Nov. 9	Bond asks trustees to apply for annual grant to purchase the Phillipps collection.
Nov. 12	Civil service writers formally organize.
Dec. 18	Lowe and others balk at civil servants' request for raises.
1873	
Feb. 6	Treasury letter asks that piecework payments to assistants for compiling catalogues be held down.
Feb. 13	Trustees recommend raises for all staff above attendants.
March 24	Second treasury letter about piecework.
April 25	Meeting of special committee of trustees (Lowe is a member) recommends only some raises.
August 2	Question in House of Commons about treasury refusal of trustees' request for raises.

Chronology

August	Lowe resigns over Post Office funds scandal; Gladstone his own chancellor of the exchequer.
Nov. 8	Bond submits to trustees first volume of facsimiles of ancient charters.

1874

Jan. 23	Disraeli goes up to London for trustees meeting. Queen dissolves Parliament; Gladstone announces an immediate election.
Jan. 26	Election held; Conservatives gain majority of forty-six in Commons.
Feb. 17	Gladstone ministry resigns; Disraeli becomes prime minister, Northcote chancellor of the exchequer, Smith financial secretary to the treasury.
March 28	Lowe and Lord Acton to special committee of trustees on salaries and finance.
April 13	Assistants at British Museum request salary increases.
May	Civil Service Inquiry Commission begins work.
June 17	Treasury grants raises for some assistants.
July 7	Classed catalogue of manuscripts completed in 108 volumes.
Dec. 24	First report of the Civil Service Inquiry (Playfair) Commission.

1875

Feb. 16	Hearings of second inquiry of Playfair Commission begin with Jones testifying.
March	Poles pamphlet printed.
March 27	Rye sends a copy of the Poles pamphlet to Mr. Brooke; has had eye operation.
May 8	Gladstone made member of standing committee of trustees.

May 14	Second report of Civil Service Inquiry Commission.
May 22	Gladstone put on trustees' subcommittee on finance.
June 14	Rye resigns.
June 26	Lowe, Somerset, Walpole on special committee of trustees on the two Playfair reports.
July	Bullen becomes keeper of printed books.
July 31	Garnett becomes assistant keeper and superintendent of the reading room.
Oct. 7	Gosse transfers to Board of Trade.
Oct.	Treasury brings up expense of catalogue.
1876	
Feb. 12	Order in Council on new civil service regulations. Gladstone resigns from standing committee.
Feb.	Arber's *Stationers' Registers*, third volume in print.
March 11	Lowe and Lord Acton on special committee of trustees to consider question of printing rather than transcribing.
March 18	Special committee reports printing too expensive.
April 24	Question in House of Commons on Museum salaries; Smith answers evasively.
May 3	Jones sends staff memorials to treasury, requesting general raises.
July 3	Another question in the House on raises for Museum employees; Northcote answers evasively.
August 1	Protests in Commons against neglect of Museum salary question.
August 12	Disraeli made earl of Beaconfield; takes seat in House of Lords.

Chronology

Oct. 4-6	American Library Association founded.
1877	
Feb.	Jones's negotiations with the treasury begin.
August	W. H. Smith becomes first lord of the admiralty; Stanley becomes financial secretary to the treasury.
Oct. 1-3	Library Association of the United Kingdom formed; Walford suggests general catalogue of English literature; committee for it formed.
Dec. 8	Jones given four months' leave for his health.
Dec. 27	Jones departs; Newton in his place.
1878	
Feb. 25	Garnett suggests printing general catalogue of the Museum to trustees; Bullen suggests early English catalogue, asked to report.
March 9	Standing committee directs Bullen to compile early English catalogue; suggests hiring copyists to transcribe entries for general catalogue.
March 25	Lingen reports on Rowland Winn's investigation, recommending typewriter.
April 13	Treasury sanctions copyists for catalogue.
April 26	Jones returns to his desk.
April	Society of Arts holds hearings on universal catalogue. Selwin-Ibbetson becomes financial secretary to the treasury.
May 25	*H.M.S. Pinafore* opens.
July 12	Library Association requests British Museum aid in compiling general catalogue of early English literature.
July 27	Jones resigns.
August 19	Bond becomes principal librarian.

Oct. 1-3	Second meeting of Library Association at Oxford.
Oct. 12	Bond's first trustees' meeting as principal librarian.
Dec.	Bond given authority to apply to Office of Works for permission to experiment with electric light for reading room.

1879

Jan. 7	Bullen reports that copyists are not satisfactory for catalogue work.
Feb. 25	Electric lighting experiments begun in reading room.
April 8	Panizzi dies.
April 21	Garnett's article on printing the catalogue in *New Quarterly Magazine*.
April	Society of Arts publishes report of its inquiry into universal catalogue.
May 10	Bond suggests to trustees that accessions be printed; is asked to draw up a report. Extended opening hours approved.
July 26	Bond reports on printing accession titles; scheme of inviting subscriptions approved.
August	Bond sends out circular announcing printing project and solicting subscriptions.
Oct. 11	Bond gets trustees' permission to apply for funds for printing.
Oct. 22	Reading room lit electrically for readers after dark.
Nov. 4	Treasury accedes to request for printing grant.
Dec. 13	Bond presents to trustees the bids on the printing project; Clowes's bid accepted.

1880

Jan.	Printing of accessions entries begins.
March 24	Disraeli dissolves Parliament.

Chronology

March	First samples of printed accessions lists shown at Library Association meeting.
April 5	Election; Liberals win large majority.
April 21	Disraeli resigns.
April 28	Gladstone forms ministry; takes the exchequer himself. Lord Frederick Cavendish is financial secretary to treasury.
May 25	Lowe to House of Lords as Viscount Sherbrooke.
June 2	Porter reports to trustees on stereotyping entries for the catalogue; permission granted to arrange for it.
July	Stereotyping tried for some titles from the general catalogue and for those of incunabula and English books printed before 1640.
Nov. 10	Major retires and Douglas replaces him as head of maps.
Nov. 11	Bullen suggests boys be hired to paste titles in catalogue volumes.
Nov. 24	Treasury agrees to boy pasters.
Dec. 30	Scheme for printing whole volumes accepted.
1881	
Jan.	Printing of whole volumes of catalogue begun. Garnett takes over the editing.
April 19	Disraeli dies; Lord Salisbury becomes leader of Conservatives.
May 2	Gladstone resigns trusteeship of British Museum.
May 10	Bullen reports early English catalogue all but finished.
June 11	Trustees order that 750 copies of Bullen's catalogue be printed.
June 20	Bullen protests shortened cleaning period planned by Bond.

July 8	Librarian of Bodleian dies; Garnett applies for the post.
Sept. 27	Garnett recalls all departmental loans in a rush because of short period allowed for verification of registers and shelf reading.

1882

Jan. 14	Bond suggests presenting copies of printed catalogue and accessions lists to public libraries; subscription price reduced.
March 25	Bond stops stereotyping program.
May 6	Lord Frederick Cavendish stabbed while walking in Phoenix Park, Dublin; Leonard Courtney succeeds him as financial secretary to the treasury.
June 24	Bullen given permission to send early English catalogue to press.
Nov. 9	Bullen reports on printing entire catalogue in alphabetical order. First volume of early English catalogue in print.
Nov. 11	Trustees decree printing of entire general catalogue to begin next year.
Nov. 25	Special meeting of trustees hears of Bond's cataloguing experiment.
Dec. 9	Bullen told to expedite revision of manuscript catalogue.
Dec.	Gladstone relinquishes exchequer to Childers.

1883

Jan. 6	Bond suggests a telephone for Museum.
Feb.	Garnett given LL.D. by Edinburgh University.
Dec.	Revision of transcribed titles finished.

1884

Jan.	Printing of catalogue from *a* to *z* begins.

Chronology

May	Bullen writes preface to early English catalogue.
June	Last volume of early English catalogue in print; three volumes bound and issued as a set.
Sept.	Treasury proposes transfer of Gosse from Board of Trade to British Museum.
Nov. 8	Garnett relieved of superintendency of reading room; Fortescue succeeds him.
Nov. 28	Bullen rejects transfer of Gosse.
November	Grant for printing increased.

1885

Feb.	Bond made Commander of the Bath.
June 8	Gladstone defeated on amendment to budget; resigns. Lord Salisbury becomes prime minister, Hicks Beach chancellor of the exchequer. Lingen resigns; Reginald Welby succeeds him at treasury.
Sept.	Garnett's "Note" on catalogue read at Lake George Conference of American Library Association.
Oct. 20	Newspaper reading room in White Wing opened.

1886

Feb. 3	Gladstone forms his third administration.
June 5	Fortescue's *Subject Index of Modern Works Added to the British Museum Library in the years 1880-1885* presented to the trustees.
July	General election; Conservatives win; Salisbury becomes prime minister, Lord Randolph Churchill chancellor of the exchequer; retrenchment begins.
1887	Sliding presses installed in Museum stacks. Northcote dies.

1888	Bond retires; Thompson becomes principal librarian. Bullen proposes amalgamating sections of entries to be sent to printer.
1890	Bullen retires; Garnett becomes keeper of printed books.
1892	Garnett is president of the Library Association. In August Gladstone becomes prime minister for the fourth time. Lowe dies.
1893	Bibliographical Society founded.
1894	Gladstone resigns March 3.
1895	Garnett is made C.B.
1897	Clowes begins to reprint early parts of catalogue.
1898	Bond K.C.B. January 1, dies January 2. Gladstone dies May 19.
1899	Garnett leaves British Museum, March 20. Article on Rudolph's blueprint process in Library Journal.
	Bullen is made C.B.
1900	General title page and preface for catalogue printed; last entries to 1881 in print. Supplement for 1882-99 accessions begun. Thompson gets approval to send complete sets of catalogue to colonies.
1905	Supplement completed.
1909	Catalogue out of print.
1931	"GK 2" begun.
1948	"GK 1" reprinted, reduced, in America.
1957	"GK 3" begun.
1967	"GK 3" in print.
1968	"Compact edition."
1979	First volumes of "BLC" in print.

Abbreviations Used in the Notes

D.N.B.   *Dictionary of National Biography*
D.O.L.B.   Director's Office letter books, British Library
Hansard   *Hansard's Parliamentary Debates*
MIN   Minutes of the standing committee of the trustees of the British Museum
M.M.   Minutes-Miscellaneous, 1861-78, Department of Manuscripts, British Library
M.S.C.   Minutes of the subcommittee of the trustees on printed books and manuscripts, British Library
P.B.L.B.   Department of Printed Books' letter books, British Library

Sections of the Letter Books of the Department of Printed Books, Beginning in 1875

I.   Minutes of the trustees relating to the acquisition of books
II.   Miscellaneous minutes of the trustees
III.   Reports relating to the acquisition of books
IV.   Miscellaneous reports, important and less important
V.   Letters from the principal librarian
VI.   Miscellaneous letters, etc.
VII.   Reports and returns of progress
VIII.   Reports of absence
IX.   Reports by assistant keepers

Notes

Introduction

1. Great Britain, *Parliamentary Papers* (Commons), 1850, vol. 24 (*Reports from Commissioners*, vol. 5), "Report of the Commissioners Appointed to Inquire into the Constitution and Management of the British Museum, with Minutes of Evidence," p. 254, answers 4207, 4209.

2. Edward Miller, *Prince of Librarians: The Life and Times of Antonio Panizzi of the British Museum* (Athens, Ohio: Ohio University Press, 1967), p. 146.

Chapter I: The Panizzian Background

1. Great Britain, *Parliamentary Papers* (Commons), 1836, vol. 10 (*Reports from Committees*, vol.4), "Report from the Select Committee on the British Museum, together with the Minutes of Evidence, Appendix and Index," pp. iv-v.

2. P.B.L.B., 1874, April 14, report of Rye.

3. Ibid., 1875, sec. IV. March 11, report of Rye.

4. D.O.L.B., vol. 43, R. Angus Smith to John Winter Jones, July 30, 1875.

5. Rye to Mr. Brooke, March 27, 1875, bound in at the front of the British Library's copy of the Poles pamphlet.

6. Stefan Poles, *The Actual Condition of the British Museum* (London: Henry Sidney Warr, 1875), p. 19.

7. Ibid., pp.28-29.

8. Rye to Mr. Brooke, April 15, 1875, bound in at the back of the British Library's copy of the Poles pamphlet.

9. P.B.L.B., 1878, sec. VI, March, T. W. Lidderdale to Bullen.

Chapter II: The Leadership of Edward Bond

1. Great Britain, *Parliamentary Papers* (Commons), 1850, vol. 24, p. 144, May 16, 1848, testimony of Sir Frederic Madden, answer 2191.

2. Ibid., answer 2325.

3. "Death of Sir E. A. Bond," *Times* (London), January 4, 1898, p. 9.

4. D.N.B., s.v. "Bond, Sir Edward Augustus." Also in Richard Garnett, "The Late Sir Edward Bond, K.C.B.," *Library* 10 (1898): 112.

5. M.M., no. 111, November 9, 1872

6. D.N.B., supp., s.v. "Franks, Sir Augustus Wollaston."

7. D.N.B., s.v. "Bond, Sir Edward Augustus."

8. "Death of Sir E. A. Bond."

9. MIN, 38:14,454-455.

10. *Library Journal* 4 (1879): 128.

11. Ibid., p. 444.

12. MIN, 41:16,227, January 6, 1883.

13. See B. McCrimmon, "Nineteenth Century Swingers: the Movable Press at the British Museum," *Library Review* 25 (1975-76): 119-23.

14. Arundell Esdaile, *The British Museum Library* (London: George Allen & Unwin [1948]), p. 138.

15. Edward Miller, *That Noble Cabinet: a History of the British Museum* (Athens: Ohio University Press, 1974), p. 254.

16. [Stride, E. A.] "A Collection of newspaper cuttings, MS. letters, photographs, and other material relating to Sir A. Panizzi, collected by E. A. Stride, 1859-1884," in the British Library, Department of Printed Books, Jones to Stride, April 25, 1880.

17. 26 Geo. 2, c. 22.

18. *Athenaeum* 71 (1879): 153.

19. P.B.L.B., 1881, sec. VI, September 27, circular.

20. Ibid., 1884, sec. II, June 14 committee.

21. Ibid., 1879, sec. VI, May 2 , "On the Supply of Books to the Library."

22. Ibid., sec. II, October 11 committee.

23. Ibid., sec. VI, January 24, Bullen to Dr. Carpenter.

24. Ibid., list dated "Sept. 1879."

25. Ibid., 1887, sec. VI, March 1, Russell Martineau to Bullen.

26. Henry Jenner, "George Knottesford Fortescue—a Memory," *Library*, 3d ser. 4 (1913): 36.

Notes

27. T. C. Skeat, "The Catalogues of the British Museum; 2. Manuscripts," *Journal of Documentation* 7 (1951): 50.

28. P.B.L.B., 1875, sec. VI, June 30, draft recommendation by Rye.

29. R. R. Bowker, "Memories among British Librarians," *Library Journal* 11 (1886): 406.

30. Jenner, "Fortescue," p. 35.

31. Beatrice Harraden, "Dr. Richard Garnett: In Memoriam," *Bookman*, June 1906, p. 92.

32. *Library Journal* 10 (1885): 189.

33. Alfred W. Pollard, "Richard Garnett," *Library*, 2d ser., 7 (1906): 252

34. David Garnett, *The Golden Echo* (New York: Harcourt, Brace, [1954]), p. 41.

35. Ernest A. Savage, *A Librarian's Memories: Portraits and Reflections* (London: Grafton, 1952), p. 151.

36. Jenner, "Fortescue," p. 35.

37. Miller, *Prince of Librarians*, p. 201.

38. Alfred W. Pollard, "Richard Garnett," *Library*, 2d ser. 1 (1899): 3.

39. Richard Garnett, *Essays in Librarianship and Bibliography* (London: George Allen, 1899: reprint ed., New York: Burt Franklin, 1970), pp. 67-86.

40. Ibid., "Public Libraries and their Catalogues," pp. 32-66.

41. Ibid., p. 66.

Chapter III: The Political Background

1. Henry Roseveare, *The Treasury: the Evolution of a British Institution* (New York: Columbia University Press, 1969), p. 192.

2. G. S. R. Kitson Clark, *The Making of Victorian England* (London: Methuen, 1962), p. 50.

3. Hansard, 3d ser., 138, col, 2192, June 18, 1855.

4. Richard Startin Owen, *The Life of Richard Owen* (New York: D. Appleton, 1894), 2:42.

5. Albert E. Gunther, *A Century of Zoology at the British Museum through the Lives of Two Keepers 1815-1914* (London: Wm. Dawson, 1975), p. 145.

6. W. F. Monypenny and G. E. Buckle, *The Life of Benjamin Disraeli, Earl of Beaconsfield* (New York: Macmillan, 1910-20), 5:400.

7. Ibid.

8. Ibid., p. 401.

9. *The Letters of Disraeli to Lady Chesterfield and Lady Bradford*, ed. the marquis of Zetland (New York: D. Appleton, 1929), 1:119, letter of June 2, 1874.

10. Hansard, 3d ser., 185, col, 496.

11. Miller, *Prince of Librarians*, p. 310.

12. *Letters of Disraeli*, 2:53.

13. John, Viscount Morley, *The Life of William Ewart Gladstone* (New York and London: Macmillan, 1880-98), 2:460.

14. Eric Alexander, third viscount Chilston, "W. H. Smith (1825-1891), the Reluctant Statesman," *Parliamentary Affairs* 13 (1960): 199.

15. Arthur Patchett Martin, *Life and Letters of the Right Honourable Robert Lowe, Viscount Sherbrooke* (London: Longmans, Green, 1893), 2:223.

Chapter IV: The Civil Service

1. Miller, *Prince of Librarians*, p. 276.

2. Hansard, 3d ser., 138, col, 2192, June 18, 1855.

3. Great Britain, *Parliamentary Papers* (Commons), 1854, vol. 27 (*Reports from Commissioners*, vol. 9), "Report on the Organization of the Permanent Civil Service, together with a letter from the Rev. B. Jowett," pp. 11, 17, 19.

4. Ibid., p. 336.

5. Asa Briggs, *Victorian People: A Reassessment of Persons and Themes 1851-67* (Chicago: University of Chicago Press, 1955), p. 77.

6. Great Britain, *Parliamentary Papers* (Commons), 1854, vol. 27, p. 336.

7. Morley, *Gladstone*, 1:649.

8. D.O.L.B., general meeting, May 11, 1872.

9. *Times* (London), August 2, 1873, p. 7.

10. Hansard, 3d ser., 117, col. 1451, August 1, 1873.

11. Ibid., col. 1453.

12. Ibid., 219, cols. 1596-97, June 15, 1874.

13. Great Britain, *Parliamentary Papers* (Commons), 1875, vol. 23 (*Reports from Commissioners, Inspectors and Others*, vol. 9), "First Report of the Civil Service Inquiry Commission, with Correspondence," pp. 10, 15.

14. Hansard, 3d ser., 227, col. 485, February 18, 1876.

Chapter V: The Treasury versus the British Museum

1. P.B.L.B., 1872, April 8, Jones to Rye.

2. D.O.L.B., vol. 19 (April-May, 1872), April 11, report of R. H. Major.

3. P.B.L.B., 1872, November 18, Jones to Rye.

4. Great Britain, *Parliamentary Papers* (Commons), 1875, vol. 23, "Second Report of the Civil Service Inquiry Commission," p. iii.

5. Ibid.

Notes

6. Ibid., p. iv.

7. P.B.L.B., 1875, sec.IV, October 6, report of Bullen.

8. Hansard, 3d ser., 228, col, 1576, April 24, 1876.

9. Ibid., 230, col, 858, July 3, 1876.

10. Ibid., 231, col. 263, August 1, 1876

11. Ibid.

12. Great Britain, *Parliamentary Papers* (Commons), 1877, vol.67 (*Accounts and Papers, Education, Science, and Art*, vol. 19), "Copy of Correspondence between the Trustees of the British Museum and the Treasury, in reference to the Salaries to be Paid to Officers of the British Museum," p. 900, no.2 February 2, 1877.

13. Ibid., p. 913, no. 7, July 2, 1877.

14. Ibid., 1878, vol. 60 (*Accounts and Papers, Charities, Ecclesiastical, Education, Science and Art*, vol. 15), "Copy of all Communications to the Trustees of the British Museum respecting the salaries to be paid to Officers and Assistants employed in that Establishment, and of all Minutes and Proceedings of the Trustees thereon subsequent to the Return of the 26th day of July 1877, Parliamentary Paper No. 332," p. 657, no 13, October 13, 1877.

15. *Athenauem* 69 (1879): 769.

16. MIN, 37:14,107-108, January 12, 1878.

17. M. S. C., 4:1825, February 25, 1878.

18. P.B.L.B., 1879, sec, V. January 13, Bond to Bullen, repeating Bullen's complaint.

19. D.O.L.B., vol. 66, April 10, 1878, report of Bullen.

Chapter VI: The Catalogue of Early English Books

1. *Athenaeum*, 23 (1850): 365-67, 390-93, 416-18, 443-46, 499-502.

2. Ibid., p. 501.

3. W. Boyd Rayward, "Systematic bibliography in England: 1850-1895," University of Illinois, Graduate School of Library Science, *Occasional Papers*, no. 84 (June 1967): 15.

4. *Library Journal* 3 (1878): 61.

5. G. W. Prothero, *A Memoir of Henry Bradshaw, Fellow of King's College, Cambridge and University Librarian* (London: Kegan Paul, Trench, 1888), p. 199.

6. P.B.L.B., 1872, May 9, Rye to Jones.

7. Ibid., 1875, sec. VI, July 14, report of Rye.

8. *Library Journal*, 2 (1878): 247.

9. Ibid.

10. Ibid., 2 (1877): 199.
11. Ibid., p. 200.
12. Ibid., 3 (1878): 296.
13. Ibid., 2 (1877): 188-90.
14. Ibid., 1 (1877): 224.
15. Ibid., 3 (1878): 188.
16. Ibid., p. 226.
17. Ibid.
18. Ibid.
19. Garnett, *Essays*, pp. 59-60.
20. Ibid., p. 59.
21. Ibid., p. 58.
22. Ibid., p. 59, footnote.
23. M.S.C., 4:1826, February 25, 1878.
24. Ibid., p. 1834.
25. *Academy* 16 (1881): 43.
26. D.O.L.B., vol. 66, March 7, 1878, report of Bullen.
27. Ibid.
28. MIN, 37:14,204, March 9, 1878.
29. P.B.L.B., 1881, sec. II, May 10, report of Bullen.
30. Ibid., October 8 and November 12 committees, report by Bullen and treasury letter.
31. Ibid., 1882, sec VI, July 11, Bond to Clowes.
32. Ibid., 1884, sec IV, June 26, Bullen to trustees, draft.
33. *Athenaeum* 77 (1885): 307.
34. *Academy* 19 (1884): 212.

Chapter VII: The Decision to Print, 1879

1. Richard Garnett, "Note on the Printing of the British Museum Catalogue," *Library Journal* 10 (1885): 201.
2. Garnett, *Essays*, p. 73.
3. Garnett, "Note," p. 202.
4. P.B.L.B., 1879, sec. II, February 8 committee.
5. *Library Journal* 4 (1879): 418.
6. Ibid.
7. *Times* (London), April 15, 1879, p. 9.
8. Garnett, *Essays*, pp. 49-51.
9. Ibid., p. 65.

Notes

10. Ibid., p. vii.
11. D.O.L.B., 1879, May 9, report of Bond.
12. MIN, 38:14, 680, May 10, 1879.
13. Ibid., pp. 14, 793-94, July 26, 1879.
14. *Library Journal* 4 (1879): 418.
15. MIN, 38:14,886, November 8, 1879.
16. Ibid., p. 14,926, December 13, 1879.
17. Garnett, *Essays*, p. 74.
18. Ibid., pp. 75-76.

Chapter VIII: Printing Begun, 1880-81

1. W. B. Clowes, *Family Business 1803-1953* (London: William Clowes and Sons [1954]), p. 45.
2. *Library Journal* 5 (1880): 79.
3. Ibid., p. 76.
4. F. J. Francis. "The Catalogues of the British Museum; I, Printed Books," *Journal of Documentation* 4 (June, 1948): 23, quoted from the foreword of Fortescue's first volume (1886).
5. P.B.L.B., 1880, sec. II, January 10 committee.
6. Ibid., February 14 committee, "Printed Catalogue-titles."
7. Garnett, *Essays*, p. 97.
8. P.B.L.B., 1880, sec VI, February 6, Bullen to Bond.
9. Ibid., sec. VII, March 3, report of Bullen.
10. Ibid., sec. IV, June 25, report of Porter.
11. Ibid., 1882, sec. II, March 25 committee.
12. R. C. Jebb, "The Book Catalogue of the British Museum," *Quarterly Review* 188 (1898): 304.
13. P.B.L.B., 1882, sec. II, December 11 committee.
14. Ibid., November 13 committee.
15. Ibid., sec. VII, "Scheme for printing volumes of the General Catalogue of Printed Books," December 30, 1880.
16. Ibid., 1881, sec. VI, January 17, Dorset Eccles to Bullen.
17. Ibid., sec. IX, January 6, monthly report of Garnett.
18. Ibid., sec. VI, January 17, Eccles to Bullen.
19. Ibid., 1880, sec. VII, "Directions for Printer."
20. Ibid., 1881, sec. IV, April 29, report of Bullen.
21. MIN, 40:15,594, April 30, 1881.
22. Ibid., p. 15,617, May 28, 1881.

23. P.B.L.B., 1881, sec. II, May 14 committee.
24. Ibid., 1886, sec. IV, November 3, report of Bullen.
25. MIN, 40:15,633-634, June 11, 1881.
26. P.B.L.B., 1881, sec. II, June 25 committee.
27. Ibid., 1881, sec VI, October 4, report of Garnett.

Chapter IX: Interim, 1882-83

1. P.B.L.B., 1882 sec. II, January 14 committee.
2. A. J. Rudolph, "The Blue Print Process for Printing Catalogues," *Library Journal* 24 (1899): 102-5.
3. P.B.L.B., 1882, sec. VI, June 29, Bond to Bullen.
4. Garnett, *Essays*, p. 66.
5. P.B.L.B., 1882, sec. IV. October 27, report of Bullen.
6. Ibid., sec. II, November 11 committee.
7. Ibid.
8. Ibid., sec. IV, "Nov.," draft by Bullen, bound in following his October report.
9. Ibid., sec. II, November 25 committee.
10. Ibid., December 9 committee.
11. Ibid.
12. Ibid., sec. IV, December 7, report of Bullen.
13. Garnett, *Essays*, pp. 82-83.
14. P.B.L.B.,1883, sec.II, February 10 committee.
15. Ibid., sec. IV, July 12, report of Bullen.
16. Ibid., sec. VI, November 30, Bullen to Bond.

Chapter X: The Third Stage, 1884-85

1. *Times* (London), January 31, 1885, p.5.
2. P.B.L.B., 1884, sec. II, November 8 committee.
3. Ibid.
4. Ibid., December 13 committee.
5. Ibid.
6. Evan Charteris, *The Life and Letters of Sir Edmund Gosse* (London: William Heinemann, 1931), p. 179.
7. P.B.L.B., 1884, sec. V, December 12, Bond to Bullen.
8. Ibid., sec. IV, November, report of Bullen.

Notes

9. Garnett, "Note," *Library Journal* 10 (1885): 202; succeeding quotations are from pp. 203-4.

10. *Times* (London), January 31, 1885, p. 5.

Chapter XI: Winding Up

1. P.B.L.B., 1888, sec. IV, December 5, report of Bullen.
2. Ibid., 1891, sec. IV, June 4, report of Garnett.
3. Ibid., 1895, sec. IV, July 22, Garnett to Thompson.
4. Ibid., November 13, report of Garnett.
5. Ibid., 1896, sec. IV. July 14, Garnett to Thompson.
6. F. C. Francis, "Meeting the Challenge: the British Museum Reprints Its Catalogue," *UNESCO Bulletin for Libraries* 11 (October 1957): 238.
7. P.B.L.B., 1898, sec. IV. September 30, report of Garnett.
8. Ibid., 1896, sec. II, October 10 committee.
9. Ibid., November 24, report of Fortescue.

Chapter XII: Epilogue

1. Garnett, *Essays*, pp. 105-6.
2. R. R. Bowker, "The Work of the Nineteenth-Century Librarian for the Librarian of the Twentieth," *Library Journal* 8 (1883): 247.
3. Francis, in "Meeting the Challenge," p. 159, cites 2¼ million, entries; Esdaile in *The British Museum Library*, p. 135, cites 4½ million.
4. Ainsworth Rand Spofford, *A Book for All Readers*, 2d ed. (New York: G. P. Putnam's Sons, 1900), p. 398.
5. W. A. Marsden, "Introduction," *British Museum: General Catalogue of Printed Books* (London and Beccles: William Clowes and Sons, 1931-53), 1:v-vi.
6. Sir Frank Francis, "Preface," *British Museum: General Catalogue of Printed Books* (London: Balding and Mansell, 1961-67), 1:[ii].

Index

Index

anese catalogues, 81; heads map section, 111; informs Dorset Eccles of his duties on second stage, 112; overruled by Bond, 113; map catalogue published, 128; receives copy of early English catalogue, 131

Duty pay, 65, 70, 75, 77, 116

Early English catalogue. *See* Catalogue of early English books

Eccles, Dorset, 112-14, 124

Eccles, Gregory W. (1837-192?), 94, 114-15, 122, 126, 131, 133

Edinburgh, University of, 41, 64

Education Committee of the Privy Council, 54

Edwards Brothers, 150

Egerton, Francis Henry, 8th earl of Bridgewater (1756-1829), 30

Electric lights in British Museum reading room, 32-33

Ellis, Sir Henry (1777-1869), 19, 21, 42

Evans, Charles John (1839-84), 124

Eyre and Spottiswoode, 105

Fellows process, 79, 80

Financial secretary to the treasury, 52-55

Fitzroy, Henry Charles, 8th duke of Somerset (1824-99), 76, 78

Fortescue, George Knottesford (1847-1912), 36, 106, 126, 132, 145

Francis, Sir Frank Charlton (1901-   ), 150

Franks, Sir Augustus Wollaston (1826-97), 32

"G K 1." *See* Catalogue, general, of printed books in the British Museum

Garnett, Richard (1835-1906): a team with Bond, 14-17; ambitious, 26; announces electric light in reading room, 33; idea for sliding press, 33, 40; calls in books for verification, 35; biographical sketch, 37-41; paper on the history of the catalogue, 41-43; proposes printing accession titles, 42; grateful to Northcote, 53; prefers subject catalogue, 86; describes Library Association meeting, 89; letter to trustees on printing, 90; kept on tenterhooks, 94; rejoices at Bond's regime, 95; article in *New Quarterly*, 98-99, 103; on Bond's negotiations, 103; duties for printed catalogue, 107, 112; says catalogue inexpensive, 107; chief editor of catalogue, 111, 129; influence rising, 112; acts hastily, 113; burdens, 114; prepares statistics,

Index

Index